The Last Fighter Pilot

THE
LAST
FIGHTER
PILOT

THE TRUE STORY OF THE FINAL COMBAT
MISSION OF WORLD WAR II

DON BROWN
with
CAPTAIN JERRY YELLIN

forewords by
Captain Jerry Yellin and Melanie Sloan

REGNERY
HISTORY
Washington, D.C.

Regnery History™ is a trademark of Salem Communications Holding Corporation; Regnery® is a registered trademark of Salem Communications Holding Corporation

Library of Congress Control Number: 2017033787

ISBN: 978-1-68451-189-1

Published in the United States by
Regnery History, an imprint of
Regnery Publishing
A Division of Salem Media Group
www.RegneryHistory.com

Manufactured in the United States of America

10 9 8 7 6 5 4 3 2 1

Books are available in quantity for promotional or premium use. For information on discounts and terms, please visit our website: www.Regnery.com.

The author is represented by MacGregor Literary, Inc.

The highlight of my life was serving my country.

—**Captain Jerry Yellin, U.S. Army Air Force,** at the seventieth anniversary reunion of the Battle of Iwo Jima, Iwo Jima, Bonin Islands, March 31, 2015

CONTENTS

CAST OF CHARACTERS

CAPTAIN JERRY YELLIN, U.S. Army Air Force—P-51 pilot from New Jersey. Seventy-Eighth Fighter Squadron Group Leader. Credited with one shoot-down. Flew last combat mission of World War II over Japan,six days after the second atomic bomb exploded over Nagasaki. Known as the "Last Fighter Pilot."

FIRST LIEUTENANT PHILIP SCHLAMBERG, U.S. Army Air Force—P-51 pilot from New York. Jerry Yellin's wingman on the final combat mission of World War II. Killed on that final mission on August 15, 1945. Last known combat death of World War II. Great-uncle of the American movie star Scarlett Johansson.

■ ■ ■

MAJOR GENERAL CURTIS E. LEMAY, U.S. Army Air Force—commanding general, XXI Bomber Command, Pacific Theatre beginning August 1944. Implemented the strategic plan for long range P-51 attacks against the Japanese homeland to be launched from Iwo Jima. Went on to become commander of USAF in Europe. Organized the Berlin Airlift in 1948. Later became chief of staff of the U.S. Air Force.

BRIGADIER GENERAL ERNEST M. "MICKEY" MOORE, U.S. Army Air Force—commanding general, Seventh Fighter Command, in command of all P-51 missions flown from Iwo Jima, Bonin Islands, against the Japanese homeland, from March of 1945 until the end of the war. Brig Gen Moore reported to Maj Gen LeMay.

COLONEL JAMES O. "JIM" BECKWITH, U.S. Army Air Force—commander, Fifteenth Fighter Group, which included the Forty-Fifth, Forty-Seventh and Seventy-Eighth Fighter Squadrons (P-51s) and operated off Iwo Jima. Col Beckwith reported to Brig Gen Moore.

COLONEL KENNETH R. "KEN" POWELL, U.S. Army Air Force—commander, Twenty-First Fighter Group, the second Fighter Group to arrive on Iwo Jima, after the Fifteenth Fighter Group. The Twenty-First Fighter Group included the Forty-Sixth, Seventy-Second, and 531st Fighter Squadrons (P-51s) and operated off Iwo Jima. Col Powell reported to Brig Gen Moore.

COLONEL BRYAN B. HARPER, U.S. Army Air Force—commander, 506th Fighter Group, the third Fighter Group to arrive on Iwo Jima, which included the 457th, 458th, and 462nd Fighter Squadrons (P-51s). The 506th began arriving on Iwo Jima May 11, 1945. Col Harper reported to Brig Gen Moore.

LIEUTENANT COLONEL HARVEY JACKSON SCANDRETT, U.S. Army Air Force—deputy group commander, 506th Fighter Group. A veteran of ninety-five combat missions and winner of the Silver Star, and credited with two shoot-downs, Lt Col Scandrett would lead the young 506th Fighter Group on a combat mission against Japan on June 1, 1945. Killed during a monster storm that struck the 506th while in flight to Japan to execute a large-scale combat mission against the Japanese homeland. Prior to his death, Lt Col Scandrett reported to Col Harper.

MAJOR JAMES M. VANDE HEY—first commanding officer of Seventy-Eighth P-51 Fighter Squadron during initial missions against Japan. Later promoted to brigadier general, U.S. Air Force. Awarded the Distinguished Flying Cross and the Bronze Star, and credited with multiple shoot-downs of Japanese aircraft. Maj Vande Hey reported to Col Beckwith while commanding the Seventy-Eighth on Iwo Jima.

MAJOR JAMES TAPP, U.S. Army Air Force—commanding officer of Seventy-Eighth P-51 Fighter Squadron in its final missions against Japan, succeeding Major James Vande Hey, and the first American ace in the air war over Japan. Credited with four shoot-downs in a single day, April 7, 1945. Maj Tapp reported to Lt Col Dewitt Spain, who succeeded Col Beckwith as commander of Fifteenth Fighter Group. Maj Tapp became one of the most prolific American aces of World War II.

FIRST LIEUTENANT BEAVER ASHLEY KINSEL, U.S. Army Air Force— P-51 pilot from San Antonio, Texas. Member of the Forty-Fifth Fighter Squadron. First P-51 pilot to lose his life operating from home base Iwo Jima. Died while in flight from suspected mechanical failure while on combat air patrol over the Pacific, March 17, 1945. Body never recovered.

MAJOR GILMER L. "BUCK" SNIPES, U.S. Army Air Force—P-51 pilot from Anderson, South Carolina and commanding officer of the Forty-Seventh Fighter Squadron. Led the first P-51 attacks from Iwo Jima against Japanese ground forces in the Bonin Islands, prior to attacks on the Japanese homeland, in March of 1945.

CAPTAIN HARRY CRIM, U.S. Army Air Force—P-51 pilot from Miami, Florida. Originally assigned to 531st Fighter Squadron, went on to become one the Air Force's greatest aces. Scored more kills than any other P-51 pilot operating off Iwo Jima. Displayed heroism in defense against Japanese Banzai attack against Twenty-First Fighter Group, evening of March 25, 1945.

CAPTAIN ERNEST THOMAS, U.S. Army Air Force—P-61 "Black Widow" pilot. Along with his crew, shot down Japanese "Betty" bomber attacking Iwo Jima, evening of March 25, 1945.

DR. GEORGE HART, U.S. Army Medical Corps, of Lake Placid, NY—flight surgeon for the Forty-Sixth Fighter Squadron. The only medical officer on duty on the night of March 25, 1945 when the Twenty-First Fighter Squadron was attacked in their tents in a Japanese Banzai Attack. With Japanese bullets flying everywhere, heroically set up an emergency surgical facility in a bulldozed depression to perform immediate surgery of Army Air Force personnel ambushed by the Japanese.

MAJOR SAM HUDSON, U.S. Army Air Force—commanding officer of the 531st Fighter Squadron. Heroically organized a three-man search-and-rescue party during surprise Japanese Banzai Attack, while under fire, along with Capt Harry Crim and Lt Harry Koke, to quickly bring shot-up pilots to Dr. Hart for Emergency Surgery. Later wounded that night when he took a Japanese grenade at point-blank range. Was relieved as CO of the 531st because of severe injuries from the grenade, and replaced by Capt Harry Crim as commanding officer.

LIEUTENANT HARRY KOKE, U.S. Army Air Force—P-51 pilot, 531st Fighter Squadron. Along with Maj Sam Hudson, and Lt Harry Crim, saved pilots ambushed in Japanese Banzai attack the evening of March 25, 1945. Even after being shot himself, continued to rescue his fellow pilots.

TECHNICAL SERGEANT PHILIP JEAN, U.S. Army Air Force—technical sergeant from Texas, assigned to the 549th Night Fighter Squadron, who on the night of March 25, 1945, during the surprise Banzai attack on the Twenty-First Air Group, displayed great heroism by grabbing a Browning Automatic Rifle and single-handedly killing eleven Japanese, while remaining under fire himself. Later lost at sea on a ship coming home from the war. Body never recovered.

FIRST LIEUTENANT DANNY MATHIS Jr., U.S. Army Air Force—P-51 pilot from Augusta, Georgia. Clemson University ROTC Graduate 1944. Served as wingman to Capt Jerry Yellin on massive air raid against Japan, May 29, 1945. Killed in a monster storm while flying on mission to attack Japan, June 1, 1945.

FIRST LIEUTENANT DICK SCHROEPPEL, U.S. Army Air Force—P-51 pilot from New Jersey. Shot down over Chichi Jima, Bonin Islands, July 3, 1945, while serving as wingman for Capt Jerry Yellin. Killed by Japanese machine gun fire while attempting to escape in an inflatable life raft.

CAPTAIN ROBERT B. RICHARDSON, U.S. Army Air Force of Irvine, Kentucky—pilot of U.S. Army OA-10 Catalina, the Army's version of the Navy's famous "Flying Boat." Landed his aircraft in the waters off Chichi Jima on July 3, 1945, under heavy enemy fire, in a daring and dangerous rescue attempt of downed P-51 Pilot Dick Schroeppel.

CAPTAIN AL SHERREN, U.S. Army Air Force—P-51 pilot from Waterloo, Iowa. Killed in action on a strafing run against the Hyakurigahara Airfield, near Tokyo, July 8, 1945.

MAJOR BILL SOUTHERLAND, U.S. Army Air Force—former commanding officer of the Seventy-Eighth Fighter Squadron. Killed in mid-air collision over Hawaii, off Haleiwa on December 9, 1943. Maj Southerland died before his squadron made it to Iwo Jima.

FIRST LIEUTENANT HOWARD EDMONSON, U.S. Army Air Force, Forty-Seventh Fighter Squadron—P-47 pilot. Killed in an accident while flying a training mission over Hawaii, Spring 1944, just before the Seventy-Eighth transitioned to P-51s. Lt Edmonson died before his squadron made it to Iwo Jima.

FOREWORD BY CAPTAIN JERRY YELLIN

United States Army Air Force

On March 7, 1945, seventy-two years from the very day that I write these words, I sat in the cockpit of a P51-D Mustang fighter plane, flying at ten thousand feet above the western Pacific, cutting a northerly course through the sunny afternoon sky toward the red-hot island of Iwo Jima, where sixty-seven thousand American Marines were still locked in battle with thousands of Japanese troops. Just three weeks beyond my twenty-first birthday, I was in many ways still the Jewish kid who grew up in Jersey, just a few years removed from many fun-filled sandlot football and baseball games with my boyhood friends in my neighborhood. I was also the same Jewish kid who had later experienced my first taste of an unfathomable prejudice sweeping the world called anti-Semitism, from some of those same friends, a bitter pill that I did not understand.

But that afternoon, over the sun-sparkled waters of the Pacific, my mind was focused only on one thing: my mission.

I had not yet experienced the war, at least not in combat. But like so many young men of my generation, I wanted to get into the fight.

I wanted to repay the Japanese for what they had done to our Navy at Pearl Harbor. Now, it was my turn.

We were the men of the Seventy-Eighth Fighter Squadron, of the Fifteenth Fighter Group, of the Seventh Fighter Command, of the U.S. Army Air Force. Our first assignment was to land on Iwo Jima, a pork-chop-shaped island of only eight square miles, in the midst of flying bullets and exploding mortars. We would become the air vanguard that would execute the final phase of the war against Japan. Our first role was to help the marines on the island by flying close-air support combat missions against twenty-one thousand Japanese troops who still occupied two-thirds of the island. Those missions would occupy the first thirty days of our mission on Iwo Jima.

Next, once the Japanese were finally defeated on Iwo Jima, our mission would be to provide fighter cover for the B-29s on long-range bombing runs from the Mariana Islands to Japan, and we would also strike and attack Japanese targets in the air and on the ground.

As my fighter approached Iwo Jima that first day, I looked out the glass canopy covering my cockpit and saw other members of my squadron, the "Bushmasters" of the Seventy-Eighth Fighter Squadron. Most of these pilots were as young as me, and many were younger. Some were in their teens, entrusted alone in the cockpit of a P-51 by their country. Most of us had not yet seen combat. Some could not even drive a car, but all were given the confidence of their country to pilot what was at the time the world's most sophisticated fighter plane. Now, that might seem incredible to ponder. But then, it was simply our duty.

None of us knew how long our mission would be. But we knew that it would be a deadly mission. We knew this from the beginning. We were all volunteers. No one was drafted into the Air Corps, later renamed the Army Air Forces. And many who volunteered had not made it this far. I had already lost the lives of five of my squadron buddies on training missions over Hawaii. The death of these five men struck hard. But there would be more loss of life. We all knew this from the beginning, but we were fully prepared to make that sacrifice for the United States.

On August 15, 1945, five months and eight days after that first flight to Iwo Jima, I was flying a combat mission over Tokyo. Six days had passed since President Truman ordered a second atomic bomb dropped, this time on Nagasaki, on August 9. For the men of the Seventy-Eighth Fighter squadron, and for all the pilots flying off Iwo Jima, we had hoped that the second bomb on August 9 would end the war and that we would never have to fly another mission in combat.

The president gave the Japanese an opportunity to surrender. We had been ordered to stand down. But August 10 passed, and still, the Japanese refused to surrender. So we were ordered back into the skies, with orders to resume striking Japanese targets-of-opportunity on the Japanese homeland, and to keep attacking until they surrendered.

My wingman that day was a nineteen-year-old Jewish kid from Brooklyn named First Lieutenant Philip Schlamberg. Phil had a life full of promise and opportunity in front of him. The valedictorian of Abraham Lincoln High School in Brooklyn, Phil's service-entrance test scores were among the very highest in the history of the Army. Because of our common Jewish heritage, and because he was one of our younger pilots, I had naturally taken Phil under my wing.

On the morning of our final flight, Phil had a premonition that he was going to lose his life. Phil had flown in combat before. But this mission had a different feel for him. I had found that whenever a pilot had a premonition, that premonition was usually right. I approached our commanding officer, Major Jim Tapp, about grounding Phil for the flight and substituting another wingman. But Phil would have none of it. He was determined to fly the mission, premonition or no premonition.

It happened shortly after we had attacked an airfield over Tokyo just after noon. We had avoided being hit by antiaircraft fire up to that point, but I was worried about Phil. I told him to stay tight on my wing, and that he would be okay. And he had done just that. We hit the field, and then climbed into a cloud embankment, with Phil flying tight in beside me. When I emerged from the clouds a few minutes later, Phil was gone. I never saw him again.

When I landed back on Iwo Jima, I learned that the war had been over for several hours, and the emperor had announced cessation of hostilities, even as we attacked that airfield. Phil and I never received the broadcast code on our radios signifying the war's end.

Phil Schlamberg, as it turned out, would take his place in history as the last-known combat death of World War II, and together, Phil and I had flown the final combat mission of the war.

History sometimes serves fascinating slices of irony. With the news emerging in 1945 of the Nazi atrocities against Jews half a world away, how ironic that the war's final mission would be flown by a couple of Jewish pilots from New York and New Jersey, and that the final combat life in the defense of freedom would be laid down by a teenage Jewish fighter pilot who had not yet learned to even drive a car.

The Last Fighter Pilot, by Don Brown, is not only my story during the final six months of the air war against Japan from Iwo Jima, but is also the story of many brave fighter pilots with whom I served, the overwhelming majority of whom are long since gone. I lost sixteen of my fellow squadron pilots during the war, men who I knew personally, and eleven of them were killed during the final phase of the air war from Iwo Jima. Most of the others have long since passed into eternity. Now, at the age of ninety-three, I am left standing to speak on their behalf. Our story needs to be told, for the sake of fully completing the history of the war.

I have said that the greatest honor of my life is to have served my country. Now, just three weeks past my ninety-third birthday, I remain standing for my fellow pilots. And still, the greatest honor of my life is to have served with these men, and to have served my country.

Jerry Yellin
Captain, U.S. Army Air Force
Orlando, Florida
March 7, 2017

FOREWORD BY MELANIE SLOAN

IN LOVING MEMORY
First Lieutenant Philip Schlamberg
United States Army Air Force

EDITOR'S NOTE—First Lieutenant Phil Schlamberg, U.S. Army Air Force, who lost his life over Tokyo on August 15, 1945, is the last known combat death of World War II, cut down after a final raid on a Tokyo air field while flying as Jerry Yellin's wingman. Phil was the youngest of ten children of Jewish-Polish immigrants in New York. He was born on the lower east side of Manhattan before moving to a poor section of Coney Island in Brooklyn, where he graduated from high school as valedictorian of his class before volunteering for the Army Air Corps. Only nineteen years old when he was killed, Lieutenant Schlamberg is memorialized on the Tablets of the Missing at the Honolulu Memorial, in the National Cemetery of the Pacific.

Melanie Sloan, the talented American film producer, actress, and talent manager, who is also the mother of the great American actresses Scarlett and Vanessa Johansson, is Phil Schlamberg's surviving niece. In this foreword, Melanie pens a loving tribute to her uncle, the man her father affectionately nicknamed "Phelly," who now takes his rightful place in history as the final combat death in the greatest war the world has ever known.

■ ■ ■

I can tell you that I used to wonder why my dad always cried when he mentioned his baby brother. They had a tremendous bond, being two out of ten children. Phil used to follow my dad in this annoying way a little brother sometimes does.

They almost drowned together in the Atlantic when they were kids growing up in Coney Island. I didn't understand the depth of his pain until after my dad died and I decided to look into my Uncle Phil's army records through the Freedom of Information Act. I found out he was a genius with the highest IQ ever measured in the Army/Air Corps, and was a guitarist, harmonica player, a comedian, a brilliant writer, and a gentle, sensitive soul.

I have a very strong bond with my dad and still feel his presence and likewise my Uncle Phil. Out of ten kids they had at least seven valedictorians and a plaque at Abraham Lincoln High School. Phil's report cards were through the roof and he got a hundred on every Regents exam. They had a very tough life. Their mom was on public assistance after my abusive grandfather deserted the family so they tried to make a few dollars for their mom by peddling ice cream on the beach while trying to evade the cops. My dad slept on the fire escape.

No one in my dad's family ever got over his death. He was the great hope of the Schlamberg Family. It killed my Grandmother Mollie.

Her baby had vanished into thin air and was declared dead after the armistice was signed with Japan. Who could make sense of it? Having a book written in his honor is a dream come true. Phil was a hero after all. He insisted on going on this last mission even with his premonition of death. I cry now sometimes thinking of my dad and Phil and the lost promise of his youth. I see him in the pure goodness and sweet smile of my son Hunter.

Despite the hard life, they all set the bar very high. I often wonder how it's possible without any guidance they were able to grow up and mature with character, strong morals, ethical standards, and a sense of purpose and duty during this time. This really was the greatest generation!

> Melanie Sloan
> New York
> March 7, 2017

The Aftermath of World War II

Like scattered hot embers popping in the glow of a dying fire pit, the long aftermath of World War II brought a smattering of skirmishes from a small handful of former enemy forces who either had not gotten the message that the war was over or, for a while, stubbornly refused to lay down their arms. This phenomenon of flickering resistance had occurred in the wake of every major war, including the American Civil War, the War of 1812, and World Wars I and II.

In Europe, for example, after the German Army had surrendered, and after the fall of Berlin, there was the strange battle for Castle Itter, where American forces actually fought alongside a ragtag group of Wehrmacht soldiers who, days before, had been the enemy of the American Army. Because the German Army had already surrendered, the Germans voluntarily joined the Americans to battle against Nazi SS forces who were trying to assassinate French dignitaries holed up in the castle. This skirmish at Castle Itter, fought on May 5, 1945, erupted five days after Hitler's suicide, and after the German Army had surrendered in Austria, Berlin, and Italy. With the surrender of the German Army and the fall of Berlin, the war was over in Europe, though the shooting erupted two days before formal surrender papers were finally signed.

In Japan, reports surfaced of disorganized Japanese forces firing at a few U.S. Navy aircraft over Japanese waters, even after the emperor had announced Japan's surrender.

Long after World War II ended, rare reports of disorganized resistance lingered for decades, with isolated Japanese soldiers fighting on in the jungles of the Pacific. Perhaps the best-known of these was Sergeant Shoichi Yokoi, who was found in 1972, in Guam, twenty-seven years after the war ended. Believing his life to be in danger, Sergeant Yokoi actually attacked his discoverers. Two years later, the last surviving Japanese soldier holding out, Second Lieutenant Hiroo Onoda, surrendered in 1974 in the Philippines.

While these minuscule pockets of resistance diminished over time, historians agree that World War II ended at noon in Tokyo, on August 15, 1945, local time (August 14 in the United States), when Emperor Hirohito took to the radio airways to announce Japan's acceptance of the terms of the Potsdam Declaration, which called for its total surrender. As the emperor began his four-minute announcement on national radio, Captain Jerry Yellin and First Lieutenant Phil Schlamberg were carrying out their final strike against a Tokyo airfield, making their historic airstrike the last known combat mission of the war, and minutes later, making Phil Schlamberg the last combat death of the war. After that, all Allied combat operations ceased, the war was over, and fate had carved the names of Yellin and Schlamberg forever into the granite annals of world history.

"Duty, honor, country: Those three hallowed words reverently dictate what you ought to be, what you can be, what you will be. They are your rallying point to build courage when courage seems to fail, to regain faith when there seems to be little cause for faith, to create hope when hope becomes forlorn."

—**General Douglas MacArthur,** General of the Army,
Supreme Commander,
South West Pacific Theatre of World War II.

PREFACE

Springtime in America

During the spring and summer of 1945 in America, a mix of joy and apprehension swept the land.

Nine months after General Dwight D. Eisenhower's "Great Crusade" for the liberation of Europe, images of American boys storming the beaches at Normandy sparked a new, electric excitement that jolted the national consciousness. The Allied victory there and the suicide of Adolf Hitler, followed by the final surrender of Nazi Germany, buoyed this optimism, for the end of the war in Europe seemed at hand. On May 8, by happenstance the birthday of new U.S. president Harry S. Truman, thousands of Americans cheered in the streets, reveling under confetti-laced showers along tickertape parade routes in Chicago, Miami, Los Angeles, and New York's Times Square as they marked the final conquest of Europe. Across the Atlantic, people were also celebrating in the great capitals of America's allies. As Winston Churchill's powerful voice pronounced absolute victory over Nazi Germany, President Truman declared VE Day to be "the greatest birthday present" that he had ever received.

The jubilant frenzy was for good reason: no more GIs would die in the Kasserine Pass, Sicily, the Ardennes, Normandy, the Hurtgen Forest, and dozens of other places throughout Europe and North Africa that, before 1942, most Americans had never heard of. Yet beneath the veneer of the public celebration, the cruel reminder of war's cost still lurked: two hundred fifty thousand Americans had perished in Europe. And apprehension remained over the prospect of an even bloodier war looming in the Pacific. As brutal as the war in Europe had been, defeating Axis ally Japan was projected to cost another one million American lives, meaning four times as many American soldiers would die in the Pacific as had been lost in Europe.

In March of 1945, as Americans from coast to coast awaited the final fall of the Nazis, a heroic group of young pilots on the other side of the world dug themselves into musty foxholes. On a lava-splashed hellhole called Iwo Jima, captured with the spilled blood of seven thousand U.S. Marines, the pilots of the Seventy-Eighth Fighter Squadron, many of whom had not yet seen combat, prepared for their final rendezvous with destiny. Their impending aerial assault on Japan would lay the groundwork for the Allies' planned invasion of the island—potentially the bloodiest ground battle the world had ever known. Flying escort to an armada of American Superfortress bombers, they would rain hell on the Japanese capital, and more Japanese would die in Tokyo from their attacks than would later die at Hiroshima. But the missions would prove deadly for these American pilots as well; in fact, many had resigned themselves to the certainty of death even before the engines on their P-51 Mustangs roared in battle. Several would perish in the cruel waters of the western Pacific as vibrant young men, their hope and future abruptly sacrificed on the altar of freedom. The survivors would continue to battle the Japanese even after the last atomic bomb blast against Nagasaki on August 9.

Their story is the final chapter of the greatest war the world has ever known, and the war's history is not complete until it is told: the heroic deeds of the Seventy-Eighth Fighter Squadron, culminating in the final combat mission flown by the man who would become the last living fighter pilot of World War II.

CHAPTER 1

The Seventy-Eighth Fighter Squadron

**Ten thousand feet above the Western Pacific—
Approaching Iwo Jima**
March 7, 1945

They sliced through a sun-splashed afternoon sky at ten thousand feet above the waters of the western Pacific. It was early March 1945, and they flew together in clusters of four known as "flights," with the smaller, four-plane groups making up larger squadrons of sixteen. Altogether, they totaled sixty-four American warplanes headed due north at a steady course of 360 degrees. The machines roared together in a thunderous chorus—a frightening and deadly sound for anyone who might be listening from the waters below.

They were the pilots of the Seventy-Eighth Fighter Squadron of the Fifteenth Fighter Group, part of the Seventh Fighter Command of the Twentieth United States Army Air Force. They sat in the cockpits of their powerful P-51D Mustangs, the most formidable fighter planes in the world at the time. With their sleek bubble canopies and aerodynamic fuselages, the planes posed a terrifying sight and packed the firepower to rain down hell from the air.

Yet despite the technological superiority of the aircraft, many of the highly trained men who flew them had not yet seen combat; they knew the war only through pictures, or War Department newsreels. Most of these pilots had arrived in Hawaii after Pearl Harbor and served in what became known as the "Pineapple Air Force," where their principal military assignment was the defense of the Hawaiian Islands against another attack by the Empire of Japan.

That attack never came.

Still, the pilots of the Seventy-Eighth had trained ad nauseam for battle, practicing simulated dogfights against one another, strafing targets on the ground and at sea, studying the tactics of their Japanese opponents, and counting the minutes till they could join the fight.

Eventually, they got their wish, which had sent them on this voyage through the sky in early March. Their destination: Iwo Jima, where many of their countrymen's lives had already been lost, with more to follow in the days ahead.

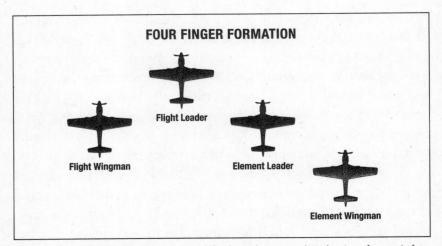

FOUR FINGER FORMATION

Flight Leader

Flight Wingman

Element Leader

Element Wingman

When viewed from above, the position of the four planes matches the tips of a man's four fingers, thus the phrase "four finger" formation.

Now on the last leg of their flight, the warbirds soared across the Pacific in their "four finger" formations, so called because when viewed from above, the position of the four planes would match the tips of a man's fingers (excluding the thumb). Out front, where the tip of the longest finger would be, flew the designated flight leader, whose role in combat was to spearhead the attack on enemy aircraft and targets on the ground. Flying to his left and a little behind was the wingman, tasked with defending the flight leader against attacks from the left side or behind the squadron. To the right of both, or the tip of the ring finger, a third pilot, known as the element leader, positioned his aircraft. The element leader, like the flight leader, assumed an offensive role—he would attack airborne aircraft and ground targets, but deferred to the flight leader when the group first opened fire. Flying behind and to his right (the tip of the "pinkie"), the element leader's wingman, just like the flight leader's wingman, played

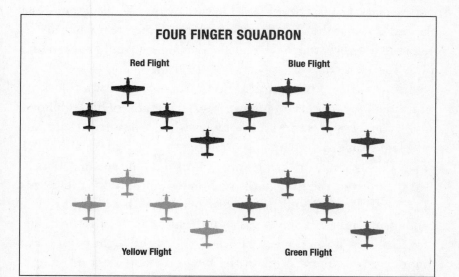

These "four finger" formations would join to create a "four finger" squadron of sixteen warplanes.

a defensive role by protecting the squadron against assault from the rear or the right flank.

This four-plane flight would join three other such flights in the air to form a sixteen-plane squadron, which provided a canopy of fighter protection for larger, slower bombers that might otherwise fall easy prey to Japanese or German fighter ambushes. Each group of four had a color designation within the squadron, usually Red Flight, Blue Flight, Yellow Flight and Green Flight.

That afternoon, flying in the element leader position of the Blue Flight, First Lieutenant Jerry Yellin sat alone in the cockpit of his P-51. His plane had been nicknamed the *Dorrie R* after a girl, Doris Rosen, with whom he'd fallen in love back home and hoped to marry as soon as the war ended. He'd met Doris on his first weekend of leave from Army flight training at Santa Ana Army Air Base in Orange County, California. Glamorous, beautiful, and slim, she was a shade taller than he, with flowing brown hair and long legs. Jerry had taped her picture onto the instrument panel in the cockpit. Yet he knew, as he glanced down at the vast, sparkling waters of the great blue Pacific, that if he were ever to see the real Doris again, he would have to find a way to survive the war.

Inside the cockpit that afternoon, it was memories that kept him company—not just of his sweetheart, but also of his childhood in Hillside, New Jersey. As a skinny Jewish kid, he'd faced sporadic anti-Semitism growing up and often felt that he had something to prove. One horrible day, with anti-Semitism on the rise in America, he'd discovered the garage of his home painted with the words "Jew" and "Nazi" and his house covered with swastikas. The vandalism happened only a few months after his twelfth birthday. Life had been normal when he went to bed the night before, but the morning brought none of the joy and excitement of being a twelve-year-old boy in the summer of 1936. Instead, Jerry and his family woke up, shocked and stunned, to images that would remain with them forever. Not long after the incident, the friends

Jerry used to play baseball with turned on him and called him a "cowardly Jew like the rest of them."

Jerry had never understood prejudice growing up. Sure, the kids in his neighborhood came in all sizes and shapes, and all had different abilities. But that did not make one kid superior to the other. Up till that fateful summer of 1936, he had been like any other boy—a decent athlete, playing second base on his school baseball team and quarter-back on the football team. He'd never given a second thought to being Jewish. His family, in fact, didn't practice Judaism. They'd never belonged to a temple nor lived in a Jewish neighborhood. What had suddenly changed now, that he would go from being just like any other boy on the block to a sudden pariah, an instant outcast that no one wanted to associate with?

He would never find the answer to that question.

But one thing he *did* know, from that point on: he would have to be stronger, smarter, work harder, and perform at a higher level than everyone else. He would have to prove strong enough to overcome any prejudice that immediately threatened to push him aside.

And, so far, he had. Those were pleasant memories: the day he received his commission as a United States Army officer, his accep-tance into flight school, the ensuing triumph of getting his wings. He'd ultimately been selected not just as a pilot, but a *fighter* pilot, placing him among the crème de la crème of aviators worldwide. Each step had culminated in the triumphant events of the last week of July, 1944, which Jerry would never forget.

At midnight on July 22, as most of the country slept, the U.S. Navy heavy cruiser USS *Baltimore* unmoored and departed San Diego accompanied by four destroyers: the USS *Cummings,* USS *Dunlap,* USS *Fanning,* and USS *Woodworth*. On reaching the Pacific, the crews shut off all navigation running lights, making it harder for enemy aircraft, ships and submarines to spot them. They set a course of 223 degrees and glided through the night without radio contact. At six a.m., four minutes after sunrise, they altered course to 270 degrees. For the next four days, as they voyaged west, the warships cut irregular, pre-arranged zigzag patterns through the water during daylight hours and reverted to total blackouts during the night, all in a heightened effort to avoid detection by the Japanese.

At nine on the morning of July 26, forward lookouts on the *Baltimore* spotted the mountains of Molokai Island, Hawaii, some fifty miles in the distance. By 10:45 a.m., the task force altered course to 221 degrees and were soon joined by an air escort from Pearl Harbor, consisting of six U.S. Navy PBM Mariners, known as "flying boats," and twelve U.S. Navy A-24 "Dauntless" dive bombers.

As the ships approached Pearl Harbor, back at Schofield Barracks— the headquarters for the United States Army in Hawaii—Lieutenant General Robert C. Richardson Jr., commanding general of all U.S. Army Forces in the Pacific, was alerted about the approaching vessels.

Richardson wanted U.S. Army aviation to show off its capabilities to the visitors and put in a call to Brigadier General Mickey Moore, commander of the old Seventh Fighter Wing (later consolidated to the Seventh Fighter Command) over at Wheeler Airfield.

Whenever a special order came down from the high brass, Moore always called on the Seventy-Eighth Squadron to get the job done; already, it had developed a reputation as the "go-to" squadron of the Seventh Fighter Command. On this occasion, Moore reached out to the squadron's commander, Major Jim Vande Hey, one of the few pilots of the Seventy-Eighth who'd been present during the Japanese attack on Pearl Harbor. Vande Hey, in turn, awarded the assignment to Major Jim Tapp, already considered by many as the best pilot in the Army.

For this task, however, Tapp could not maximize his impressiveness as an air showman without a wingman. Tapp had his pick of anyone in the squadron to fill the role. But the symbiotic relationship between a pilot and his wingman in combat or situations involving high-risk aerobatics—where a millisecond of indecision could bring about catastrophe—meant that the trust factor between the two pilots had to be unshakable. All too often, pilots got killed in air shows because of that millisecond of indecision. Knowing the importance of precision in his assignment, that life or death could hang in the balance, and that top military brass in the Pacific would be watching, Tapp settled on the skinny kid from New Jersey for the assignment.

"Yellin, suit up. We're going up," Tapp had ordered. "Get on my wing, and don't get off. If you get off, you'll be sorry you ever flew."

That's all Jerry was told. But he knew the best pilot in the Army had selected him to be his wingman, and he also realized that, whatever they were doing when they got in the air, it was going to be high pressure.

The two pilots fired up their engines and lifted off into the blue Hawaiian skies. Cutting northeast, they were over the Pacific within a matter of seconds. The flight out to the USS *Baltimore*'s location lasted about fifteen minutes, and when they arrived, with Jerry tight on Tapp's left wing, they buzzed in close over the top of the ship, looped up into the sky, turned, and proceeded to fly a number of tight aerobatic maneuvers.

They were dangerous, impressive stunts. The pilots executed "lazy eights," whereby the aircraft, flying in tight formation, cut two large, swooping, 180-degree turns in the sky—the first of many "figure eights" they drew just off the starboard side of the ship. The duo performed an assortment of loops and rolls in perfect symmetry, with Jerry flying off Tapp's wing the whole time. After finishing the acrobatics, the pilots turned a wide circle in the air, and again, with Jerry on Tapp's wing, flew a tandem salute across the ship before heading back for Schofield.

At 2:25 p.m., meanwhile, the *Baltimore* arrived at the entrance of Pearl Harbor, where she stopped to receive a boarding party of high-level military officers, including Admiral Chester Nimitz, the commander-in-chief of the U.S. Pacific Fleet. If the high-ranking officers boarding the ship didn't suggest that something unusual was occurring, the sight of sailors donned in summer white uniforms and manning the rails on every U.S. warship should have been a clue. As the *Baltimore* entered the protected waters of Pearl Harbor, she hoisted the blue flag of the president of the United States up onto her main.

The news traveled faster than the wind: Franklin Delano Roosevelt, the commander-in-chief, had made a surprise visit, courtesy of the U.S. Navy.

The telephone lines and the gossip circuits on Oahu Island ignited. When the news reached Schofield, Jerry finally realized he had flown a demonstration for the president of the United States (Tapp had been informed of Roosevelt's presence when assigned the mission). It was a proud, defining moment for the young pilot.

Now, nine months later, he was flying toward what would become his corner of this great war. Despite the risk, he had confidence in his abilities—an attitude that served fighter pilots well when they engaged in combat. Aside from skill, no trait was more valuable than the mindset they carried into battle, which gave them a certain swagger. The great fighter pilots possessed a killer instinct, a certain thirst for aggression, to get the job done. Fearlessness in facing death was a must. Jerry, for his part, had both the talent *and* the motivation. He'd become a fighter pilot to kill Japanese soldiers, to exact vengeance on them for attacking his country and killing his countrymen, and to defend freedom. And that's exactly what he was going to do.

There! Off in the distance!

Rising from the watery horizon surfaced Jerry's first visual of Iwo Jima: the distinct, jagged, dark outline of Mount Suribachi, towering 555 feet up above the water. Sixteen days had passed since U.S. Marines landed on its beaches; even now, however, as Jerry piloted his Mustang toward the island, it remained infested with the enemy. Although the Marines had secured a beachhead, the Japanese controlled two-thirds of the eight-mile island, which meant that Jerry's squadron could very well take ground fire while landing.

Ten minutes later, the island had morphed from a single peak into a panoramic view. Some Marines who fought there described the island's shape as a "large, gray pork chop." In times of peace, it would be covered with green vegetation. But the U.S. Navy—with some assistance from the U.S. Army Air Force—had bombed and shelled the hell out of the island for eight months before the Marines landed on February 19, 1945. Their invasion had been a long time coming— it existed in planning and operational stages for well over a year, starting in February of 1944 when American B-24 and B-25 bombers had blasted the islands for seventy-four consecutive days. In the ten days prior to the Marines hitting the beaches, the naval bombardment intensified. As a result, the island out in front of the *Dorrie R* now appeared gray, its vegetation burned off by naval gunfire. Indeed, it looked as it was for many: an island of death, not of life.

As the pilots of the Seventy-Eighth approached Iwo Jima from the south, maintaining their cruising speed of 360 miles per hour, their vision of the enemy-controlled areas to the north was blocked by Mount Suribachi, which rested on the island's southern tip. In February of 1945, after the Marines had established their beachhead on the southern third of the island, the Associated Press released a drawing to illustrate what the Marines had captured and what the Japanese still held.

Jerry and his peers had studied navigation charts similar to the AP map. They knew that, once they cleared Mount Suribachi, they would descend quickly and try a bull's-eye landing onto the dirt air-field at the base of the mountain. The descent had to be quick to avoid enemy fire.

As they drew nearer the island, Major Jim Vande Hey, the squadron commander, broke out into landing formation, leading the Red Flight ahead of the other groups. Next came the Blue foursome; Jerry, as element leader, fell in line as the third plane in the landing pattern. Behind them, the Green and the Yellow Flights followed suit.

Inside the *Dorrie R*'s cockpit, Jerry began his pre-landing procedure.

Increase prop speed to twenty-six hundred RPM: check.

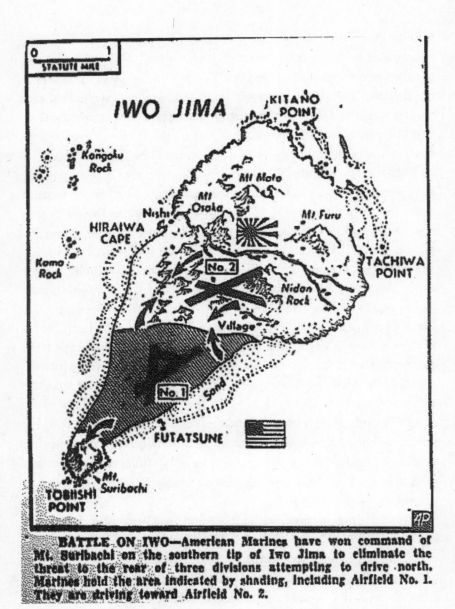

BATTLE ON IWO—American Marines have won command of Mt. Suribachi on the southern tip of Iwo Jima to eliminate the threat to the rear of three divisions attempting to drive north. Marines hold the area indicated by shading, including Airfield No. 1. They are driving toward Airfield No. 2.

This Associated Press drawing, released in February of 1945, illustrates what the Marines had captured and what the Japanese still held in the initial stages of battle.

Retard throttle to check landing gear: check.
Airspeed 250 miles per hour.
Airspeed 200 miles per hour.

As it dropped to 170 miles per hour, Jerry pushed the landing gear handle into the DOWN position. He waited a few seconds, then retarded the throttle to check his warning lights. Excellent. He lowered first his landing gear, then the plane's flaps, and dropped airspeed to just below 165 miles per hour.

The plan was to buzz the field in groups of four abreast to get a visual feel for the landing area, then pull up for a quick half-loop, line up with the airfield, and land the plane.

The Red Flight went first. Jerry watched from above, in a holding pattern, as the first wave of P-51s lined up abreast and swooped down over the field. They pulled up, conducted a quick half-loop, and Tapp then brought his plane onto final approach for landing.

Touchdown.

The second aircraft followed. So did the third, while the Blue Flight lined up for its pre-landing buzz of the airfield. Jerry pushed forward on the stick, and the Mustang nosed down. Flying over the airfield, Jerry observed the planes that comprised the Red Flight being moved out of the way. He could also see other P-51s that had landed yesterday in the first wave of fighters to arrive on the island. As he swung around in a half-loop and lined up for final approach, he didn't have time to think he'd also just gotten his first glimpse of the place where he might die.

No, there was no time to ponder any of that. Right now, he needed to get the *Dorrie R* on the ground—and fast.

The Blue Flight descended in a straight line for landing and spaced fifteen to twenty seconds apart, a margin that left no room for error. Jerry nosed the Mustang down, keeping his eyes on the airfield and the tail of the plane in front of him.

Eight hundred feet...

Six hundred feet...

Four hundred feet…

Two hundred feet…

The Mustang in front of him touched down.

Ten seconds to landing.

Five seconds.

As he flew across the end of the dirt runway, slowing the plane's air speed to one hundred miles per hour and just ten feet off the ground, Jerry pulled back on the stick, feathering the nose up as the plane dropped. A second later, he touched down. It was a good landing—no bounce on contact—and the plane raced forward on the runway.

Thank God, he thought.

Jerry raised his flaps and cut the booster pumps, then opened the oil and coolant shutters. At the end of the airstrip, he waited until the Mustang's propeller stopped spinning and then turned the ignition switch off.

When he opened the glass-bubble canopy over the cockpit, it hit him: the most putrid, nauseating stench he'd ever inhaled. Battling a powerful instinct to vomit all over himself, Jerry looked over and saw the source of the odor: dead Japanese, piled up six to eight feet along the side of the runway. Many were mutilated from battle. Some, who had been killed more recently, still oozed with blood. Others rotted in the warm mid-afternoon sun, swarmed by thousands of flies and maggots. The bodies would be pushed into mass graves when the Marines got around to it.

Meanwhile, if the overpowering stench of death wasn't baptism enough into the horrors of a war zone, the immediate orders being snapped at the pilots drove home the reality.

"Secure your planes!"

"Stow your gear!"

"Stay low!"

"Grab a shovel and dig a foxhole. Keep your heads down, men!"

Nothing had prepared Jerry for this. The graphic nightmare flooded his lungs, his stomach, and his conciousness.

"Lieutenant, get out of the plane!" a voice called through the chaos. "We're in a war zone. We've gotta get you to a foxhole!"

CHAPTER 2

The First Night in Hell

Iwo Jima
March 8, 1945

That night, Jerry tried to fall asleep as the odor of rotting dead bodies filled his nostrils. He was lying in a foxhole he'd dug for himself using tools the Marines had supplied. His orders now were to get some shuteye. As a pilot, he needed to stay razor sharp; the Seventy-Eighth and their sister squadrons in the Fifteenth Fighter Group had been told that, at sunrise, they would be back in the air, providing support to the bombarded Marines. Sleep was imperative.

But it wasn't just the overwhelming stench of death that tormented Jerry as he lay flat on his back in the dirt. Thousands of flies swarmed above his head, buzzing like miniature fighter planes as they flew among the dead bodies on which they feasted. Jerry tried swatting away the insects with his hand, but to no avail. There were too many.

There was also the gunfire. It came from everywhere—rifle fire, pistol fire, the discharge of machine guns, exploding grenades, and the whiney pitch of mortars launching, flying through the air, and exploding on contact. Jerry could hear the warning call of

Marines—"*Incoming!*"—when mortar fire from the Japanese entered the area. The earth around him shook from the fire, while the noise filled his ears.

But perhaps worst of all was the sound of men screaming, as dying moans escaped their bodies. With their last breath, they cried to God or begged for their mothers.

The constant uncertainty of Jerry's own fate pressed on him. At any moment, a mortar round could land in his foxhole, and there wasn't a damn thing he could do about it. His life through the night depended on factors he could not control.

Like hell he'd be able to sleep.

The Marines had been living through this nightmare for two weeks already. Americans back home had seen the iconic black-and-white image of their countrymen raising the flag on Iwo Jima. The picture had been snapped by photographer Joe Rosenthal on February 23, 1945. But by the time Jerry landed on the island just twelve days later, two of the six men who pushed the flag into the sky were already dead. Even now, a final victory on Iwo Jima was still weeks away, and before it came, a third soldier depicted in that memorable photograph would pay the ultimate price.

And yet, despite its shocking depiction in the mountains of dead Japanese and the cries of the Marines that pierced the air around him, the devastation of war was not wholly new to Jerry. Already, before arriving at Iwo Jima, he'd witnessed the death of fellow pilots. In December of 1943, his former commanding officer, Major Bill Southerland, was killed in a mid-air collision over Haleiwa after his plane collided with another plane piloted by Jerry's squadron mate, Howard Edmonson. Though Edmonson was at fault, he bailed out and survived. Six months later, after Edmonson received what appeared to be shocking news from home, he flew his P-47 into the ocean off the coast of Hawaii. To this day, it is not clear whether the crash was accidental or on purpose. More likely, it was accidental, since Edmonson had been drinking the previous night, which may

"Raising the Flag on Iwo Jima"—This iconic, Pulitzer-winning image was captured by Joe Rosenthal on February 23, 1945, the fifth day of the battle. *AP Images*

have affected his coordination. Either way, his death shocked the squadron, and was especially hard to swallow, as he left a wife and a family to mourn him. Edmonson was the first of his fellow pilots that Jerry lost in the war.

The nightmare reality was that he likely wouldn't be the last. Here, on this island, death seemed the norm, not the exception. Jerry's first night in the foxhole may as well have been a first night in hell. The ground itself, because of volcanic activity deep beneath the surface, emitted heat into the foxholes, which could make them uncomfortable to lie in for long periods of time. The very name Iwo Jima meant "Sulfur Island" in Japanese, and with good reason—volcanic sulfur covered the island, and the hot sulfur springs ran all under the surface. The underground volcanic activity made Iwo Jima hotter than most tropical islands, and at night, the heat from the open foxholes, as it rose into the cooling evening air, produced at times a ghost-like mist.

And that eerie mist carried another drawback: it gave cover to Japanese infiltrators seeking to slip into the Americans' camp and slit their throats while they slept. Jerry and the rest of the Seventy-Eighth had already been warned by the Marines about the Japanese: "They're not *on* the island. They're *in* the island." The Japanese had spent months burrowing an interior network of secret tunnels throughout this eight-square-mile lava lump in the Pacific. In fact, more than twenty-five thousand Japanese soldiers crammed under the surface and caves of an island that was only two miles at its widest point. They had been abandoned by the Imperial government and ordered to fight to the death. Even in the small space controlled by the Marines, such secret tunnels threatened the safety of the Americans. The Japanese were fond of popping up out of the ground unannounced, under cover of darkness inside the American lines, and committing mass murder before slipping back under the earth. They'd jump into American foxholes, cut American throats, then disappear without ever having been seen. The Marines had already flushed out many of the tunnels around the airfield where Jerry's foxhole was located, but there were no guarantees.

At this moment, Jerry felt defenseless. Put him in the cockpit of a fighter—where he controlled the most lethal killing instrument in the war—and he could soar into the heavens and do some good. Here, in a foxhole, he was powerless. Sure, he had his sidearm with him—the pilots had undergone small weapons training and were prepared to fire on the enemy in the event of a shoot-down. But a pilot also needed to be in control of his situation. Of all things Jerry hated in his current position, he hated the lack of control most of all. In the cockpit, he had control of his aircraft, control of his guns and bombs, and, most importantly, control over the enemy.

How he wished he could go jump in the cockpit of the *Dorrie R* right now, crank the engine, and bring hell to the Japanese.

Jerry's mind drifted to his aircraft's namesake. He closed his eyes and allowed himself to think of Doris Rosen. Even here, he could see her long, flowing hair bouncing off her shoulders, and that irresistible, starry gaze as she looked into his face. A soldier needed hope—hope for something, or someone, to come home to. At this moment, she gave him hope. The thought of her allowed him a brief smile, even in the midst of a smoldering hellhole.

More explosions and gunfire brought Jerry's eyes wide open again. He grasped his pistol grip, if for nothing more than a small semblance of comfort.

Slowly, the truth dawned: there would be no sleep tonight.

Hopefully, he'd be sharp enough to fly in the morning.

CHAPTER 3

A Graveyard for Bombers and the Need for Iwo Jima

The Mariana Islands
November 1944

In any hellhole, the question eventually becomes, "why?"

Why were American troops fighting in places and under conditions that could pass for the hottest, dirtiest, deadliest, and most deplorable on the planet?

Why Iwo Jima? Why had Jerry and his fellow pilots flown their P-51s over the waters of the western Pacific and, risking life and limb, executed a pinpoint landing on a small island in a ferocious war zone?

The answer: the United States needed a mid-ocean landing strip for its fighter pilots, and Iwo Jima just happened to be at the right place. Capture it, and the airstrips already built by the Japanese become available to the American P-51s that needed to protect B-29 bombers trying to strike the Japanese homeland.

Before the Marines even started their offense against Iwo Jima, however, they'd had to capture the Mariana Islands, which lay in the Pacific to the southeast of Japan and southwest of Hawaii. Named for the Spanish Queen of Austria, Mariana, who lived in the seventeenth century, the islands remained under Spanish jurisdiction until the Spanish-American war, when Spain ceded control of Guam, the largest of the Mariana Islands, to the United States in 1898. Of the sixteen islands making up the Mariana chain, only four were populated: Guam—the best-known island of the Mariana chain—Saipan, Tinian, and Rota, all of which had been captured by the Japanese soon after Pearl Harbor.

Upon taking back the Marianas, the United States had used the island to stage aviation assets for future use against Japan. In January of 1945, some two months before they would first land on Iwo Jima, Jerry and his squadron mates from the Seventy-Eighth boarded the USS *Sitkoh Bay,* a small "jeep" carrier launched less than a year earlier and named for a tiny, idyllic bay in Southeastern Alaska. It was lightly armed and largely defenseless against enemy submarines. The men were jammed on board the ship with their planes, which were greased down to protect their wings, cowlings and fuselages from the corrosive effects of the salty sea. Only after the pilots boarded did they learn their destination was Guam.

The *Sitkoh Bay* had cut a two-week westerly course of four thousand miles across the Pacific, alone and unprotected except for the thirty-seven light antiaircraft guns positioned around her deck. Had a Japanese sub spotted the ship, she surely would have gone down, and—like the crew of the USS *Indianapolis,* which was torpedoed several months later—left her passengers to drown or be mauled by sharks.

But on this trip, the *Sitkoh Bay* got lucky. No Japanese submarine spotted her. And for the men of the Seventy-Eighth, the cross-ocean voyage would prove their last taste of anything with a semblance of luxury. The commanding officer of the *Sitkoh Bay* and his crew took it upon themselves to treat the Army aviators like deserving kings. This included steak dinners, linen sheets, nightly movies, and volleyball courts on the flight elevator.

Once they arrived in the tropical climate of Guam, the luxury— if one could call it that—ended. Under sweltering sunshine, the P-51s were unloaded, cleaned up, washed down, and matched with their pilots. Located on the earth's thirteenth parallel, with year-round temperatures in the eighties, the island's warm breezes and tropical beauty painted an eerie, surrealistic contrast to the bloody war zone around it. This brief respite on Guam was the pilots' last rest before facing the scourge of war and inhaling the stench of death. Within a few days, Jerry and his comrades flew their Mustangs 120 miles north to Saipan, where they waited for the Marines to seize control of Iwo Jima. From there, the P-51s could begin assaulting Japan itself.

Saipan, which the Japanese considered a last geographic line of defense to the homeland, had fallen to Marines on July 9, 1944, just one month after Normandy. Her sister island, Tinian, fell three weeks later, on August 1, 1944. These tropical islands—Guam, Saipan, and Tinian—would become crucial as staging bases in the final air wars against Japan. In fact, the atomic bomb that drove the final nail in Japan's coffin would be flown from Tinian.

To prepare for the eventual invasion of the Japanese homeland, the Allies' battle plan resembled that used for the invasion of Europe. The first step would involve a massive, strategic bombing campaign of Japan over a number of months to soften the enemy's resolve before the first stage of a ground invasion around November 1, 1945. The pre-invasion air war would involve bomber strikes on the Japanese homeland from the Mariana Islands, with fighter cover launched from Iwo Jima. B-29s could strike from fourteen hundred miles away, but fighter planes—notably the P-51s needed to protect those bombers—did not have long-distance striking ranges. Consequently, America needed a base for her fighter planes closer to Japan.

That's where Iwo Jima came into play. It was 759 miles south of Tokyo, about half the distance between the Japanese capital and the American bomber bases in the Marianas, making it the perfect location for a fighter base. The fighter planes' smaller fuel tanks could make the fourteen-hundred-mile round-trip flight, unlike the twenty-eight-hundred-mile round-trip flight from the Marianas. From Iwo

Jima, the P-51s could launch and accompany the bombers flying from Saipan, Guam, and Tinian to Japan. Thus, controlling Iwo Jima became key to the U.S. war effort in the Pacific.

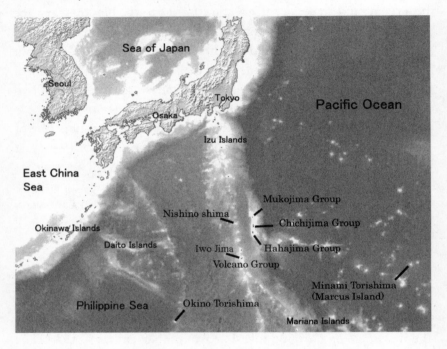

Controlling Iwo Jima became key to the U.S. war effort in the Pacific.

The man who'd been chosen to lead this air war against Japan was General Curtis LeMay, a native of Columbus, Ohio, who'd eventually serve as the vice-presidential running mate for Governor George Wallace on the American Independent Party ticket in the 1968 presidential election. LeMay had begun his career with the U.S. Army Air Corps (renamed the U.S. Army Air Forces in 1941) and made history as the general who directed U.S. air operations during the Berlin Airlift. A brilliant pilot and military aviation tactician, he'd reached full-bird colonel when he took command of a new B-24 bomber unit in England during World War II. Without adequate fighter escorts in

1943, LeMay's bombers sustained heavy losses on dangerous and daring missions flown deep over Germany as they attempted to take the war to the Nazis more than a year before the Normandy invasion.

What LeMay learned during those missions to Germany proved prescient for his later command in the Pacific. A saying in American football applied to the punting team warns, "Don't out-kick your coverage." It's so worded because, if the punter kicks the ball too far downfield ahead of the punt coverage team, the other team can catch the ball and start to make a maneuver before the punt coverage unit gets downfield to make a tackle. That football saying also applied to the early doctrine of aerial warfare during World War II. The bomber was the football, and the fighter planes were the punt coverage unit. If a bomber flew out over enemy territory ahead of its fighter coverage, bad things could happen. Thus, fighter aircrafts like the well-known British Spitfire and the incomparable American P-51 Mustang were designed to protect larger bombers on their missions deep over hostile territory.

But when selecting bombing targets tucked snugly away in Germany, a new reality emerged. Though the bombers—such as the B-17, the B-24, and later the B-29—were bigger and slower than their fighter escorts, they also had one major advantage: their fuel tanks were much larger, meaning the bombers could penetrate deeper than their fighter escorts into enemy territory to deliver their payload (provided they could make the trip without being shot up—or shot down). Thus, the real danger to the bombers came when the fighters had to turn back on long-range bombing runs because of smaller fuel supplies. Though most bombers were armed with .50-caliber machine guns, because of the plane's larger size and diminished maneuverability, a bomber's capacity to defend itself was compromised without fighter escorts. This dynamic left the bomber pilots with a choice: use the superior fuel tanks to their advantage and penetrate deeper into enemy territory without fighter protection, or take the safe path and turn back when their fighters did.

Early in the air war against Germany, American bombers from the Eighth Air Force often out-flew their fighter coverage, increasing their vulnerability against enemy aircraft and antiaircraft fire. Doing so required great skill and bravery. And the American bomber pilot who most distinguished himself for flying into harm's way with no fighter protection was Curtis LeMay.

His signature mission came in August of 1943. Ten months before the grand invasion of France, the Allies commenced a strategic carpet-bombing campaign of Germany as a prelude for the ground invasion. The air campaign was designed to soften enemy resistance on the ground, thus giving Allied forces a slightly safer chance to march towards Berlin. However, at the time, the United States had no fighter aircraft capable of accompanying the bombers on these long-range missions. Therefore, bomber pilots knew from the beginning they would be out-flying their fighter coverage and thereby exposing themselves to German fighter attacks.

On August 17, in broad daylight, LeMay flew deep into Germany without fighter coverage in what became known as the *Schweinfurt-Regensburg* mission. The targets were military aircraft factories and ball-bearing factories (ball bearings were used in military ground vehicles, such as tanks, and other machines). A total of 376 B-17 bombers were scheduled to fly without fighter escort. To compensate for lack of U.S. fighter coverage, LeMay devised a plan to split the bombers into two separate groups, thus dividing (and thereby weakening) the enemy's own fighter coverage. LeMay would command the Fourth Bombardment Wing on the most dangerous leg of the mission—a strike against Regensburg, where the Americans would target factories that produced German Messerschmitt fighter aircraft. The other U.S. air commander, Colonel Bob Williams, would lead the First Bombardment Wing on a mission over Schweinfurt to attack ball-bearing plants crucial to the German war effort. Though both were high-risk endeavors, the Messerschmitt factories would be more fiercely defended, thus making them more dangerous targets.

The mission proved highly successful, despite its cost. The Eighth Air Force lost sixty B-17 bombers, shot down by German antiaircraft fire and fighter fire. Another ninety-five bombers were heavily damaged. The Germans lost only twenty-seven fighter aircraft—less than half the number of bombers lost by the Eighth Air Force—but the mission rendered a short-term blow to the German war effort by delaying production of fighter aircraft for weeks and creating brief shortages of ball bearings needed to operate Nazi war machines.

The mission ultimately became the model for the planned long-range bombing of Japan, but LeMay learned from its mistakes, too. In attacking Japan, he would demand fighter support, and a mid-ocean base from which those fighters could be launched. That was Iwo Jima.

CHAPTER 4

Assessing the Threat

1944

LeMay arrived in the Pacific region the summer before the United States had secured a foothold on Iwo Jima. In August of 1944, two months after the great Allied invasion at Normandy, the American high command had transferred him to the China-India theater to assume control of the Twentieth Bomber Command in China. China was a more desirable location for U.S. forces than the Mariana Islands, since it was much closer to Japan. But it quickly became apparent that setting up strategic bomber bases in eastern China to attack Japan posed logistical issues that rendered the entire setup impractical.

Part of that had to do with the vicious beating the Japanese had inflicted on the Chinese in the decade prior to LeMay's arrival in the region. While Americans marked the Japanese attack on Pearl Harbor as the moment in which the United States essentially entered the war, the first taste of Japanese aggression in World War II for the Chinese occurred ten years earlier when Japan invaded Manchuria on September 18, 1931. Sometimes referred to as "Northeast China," Manchuria occupied the far northeastern section of China and was separated from

Japan by the Sea of Japan. When the Japanese invaded Manchuria in 1931 and the Chinese did not oppose the invasion, Japan declared Manchuria to be an independent state. The independence was in name only, of course, for the area remained under Japanese control and later became a convenient staging base for Japanese incursion into China.

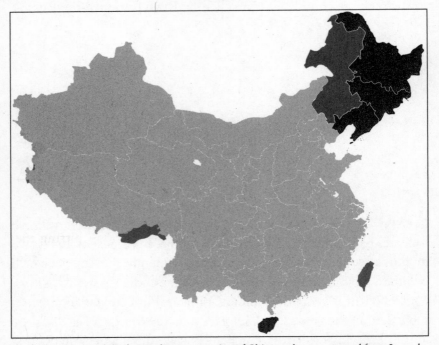

Manchuria occupied the far northeastern section of China and was separated from Japan by the Sea of Japan.

The Japanese, however, wanted Manchuria for reasons other than its military positioning. Japan was a volcanic archipelago, consisting of over sixty-eight hundred islands. Most of these islands were tiny and uninhabitable, with four of them—Honshu, Hokkaido, Kyushu, and Shikoku—making up over ninety-seven percent of the Japanese landmass. As an island nation, Japan needed more space and natural resources, and Manchuria offered rich ones, including minerals, forest, and land for agricultural purposes. The Japanese homeland was also becoming crowded, and owning Manchuria would give the exploding population somewhere to expand.

Manchuria itself had been the subject of competing claims from several nations over the years. Though culturally Chinese, large portions of the area had been controlled by Russia prior to the Russo-Japanese War, fought between February of 1904 and September of 1905. The conflict pitted the ambitions of Russia against Japan for control of both Manchuria and Korea. For the Japanese, both countries provided natural geographic buffers separating them from imperialist Russia, which Japan accused of having expansionist territorial ambitions. They may very well have been correct. The Russians had already expanded their massive Eurasian holdings to warmer waters in the Pacific and constructed two valuable railways in the region, the Chinese Eastern and the Manchurian Railway, revealing their intent to assert a powerful influence in East Asia.

But soon after the establishment of the Manchurian Railway—paid for by the Russians—the Boxer Rebellion arose, pitting the uprising of Chinese nationalists against "foreign influence" and Christian missionaries. The "Boxers," a group of Chinese peasants who attacked and killed Christian missionaries and Chinese Christians across China during 1899 and 1900, were supported in the massacre by the Qing government and the Chinese Imperial Army. In response to the Boxers, an ironic alliance of eight "allied" nations (known as the "Eight Nation Alliance") joined together in China to suppress the rebellion. The alliance members were Japan, Russia, Britain, France, the United States, Germany, Italy, and Austria-Hungary—many of which, in just a few short years, would be pitted against one another in two of history's bloodiest wars. Yet, for a brief, one-year period, they came together in what proved a short-lived alliance. The first post-alliance rupture occurred between Japan and Russia, triggered in large part by Russian troop buildups in Manchuria.

Already, by the time of the Boxer Rebellion in 1900, Russia had sent one hundred seventy-seven thousand troops to the region to protect its railways under construction. This massive troop movement, even during the period of the "Ironic Alliance," strengthened Japan's worst fears. War erupted between the two empires on February 8, 1904. Though not known about by most Americans, the Russo-Japanese War would prove to be among the bloodiest in history. The battle of Mukden involved six hundred thousand combatants and was the largest battle fought by an army organized along modern lines in Asia until World War II. Despite the tragic casualties incurred, Japan managed to trounce the Czar's eastern army and navy and do so quickly, thereby upending a long-held international notion that Asians were an inferior race incapable of competing with Caucasian nations.

After the Japanese soundly beat the Russians, U.S. President Teddy Roosevelt stepped in to personally mediate the end of the conflict. The war ended on September 5, 1905, with the signing of the "Treaty of Portsmouth," named for the Portsmouth Naval Shipyard in New Hampshire where Roosevelt helped broker and negotiate the treaty that officially suspended the war. Following its defeat, Russia transferred control of the Liaodong Peninsula—which included part of Manchuria—to Japan. Russia had just officially lost its warm water port and had also became the first European power in modern history to lose a war to an Asian power. One of the great spoils grabbed in the victory by the Japanese was the Russian-built South Manchuria Railway Company, which Japan soon made its chief instrument for the economic exploitation of Manchuria. Ultimately, however, the shocking victory marked Imperial Japan's arrival on the stage of world powers. And she wanted more.

And so, in 1931—ten years before Pearl Harbor—Japan launched a full-scale invasion of Manchuria (since victory against the Russians had only ceded them military control of the part of the region known as the Liaodong Peninsula). It could be argued that date—September 18, 1931—marked the real start of World War II, as it saw the massive mobilization of the ferocious Japanese war machine. The 1929 world-wide depression had hit Japan hard: within the country, there was a perceived need for the additional natural resources they believed could be found in Manchuria. China, meanwhile, would not trouble their ambitions, for that country was four years into civil war. In fact, when Japan first invaded Manchuria, Chiang Kai-Shek, China's nationalist leader, adopted an appeasement strategy in order to focus on defeating the communist uprising.

By 1933, the Imperial Japanese Army, marching under the guise of the Manchukuo Army, launched an invasion of northern China and moved into China's northern Jehol province, which adjoined the Manchurian border. The Japanese troops only stopped their march short of the former Chinese capital Peking when a last-minute truce was arranged. The truce, of course, favored the Japanese in a big way. Under its terms, Chinese troops were barred from all areas in China now occupied by the Japanese Army.

Then, in the spring of 1936, the Japanese transferred the First Division of the Kwantung Army to Manchuria, the largest infantry division in the army. Extremist officers in the army also revolted against the Japanese emperor's chief advisers, intent on removing obstructionists who opposed military expansionism. The first coup attempt occurred in Tokyo on February 26, 1936.

Now referred to as the "February 26 Incident," these conspirators assassinated two of Emperor Hirohito's key advisers. Other rogue army members surrounded the Japanese Foreign Office and held much of Tokyo hostage for three days. The insurgents captured the minister of war, the governor-general of Korea, and the commander of the Kwantung Army, which was the largest and most prestigious command in the Japanese army. The coup attempt failed only when the Army High Command refused to support the mutineers. The leaders of the mutiny were persuaded to commit suicide to avoid a trial that would have embarrassed the Army. However, in a greater sense, the coup attempt succeeded, as the Army would end up asserting even more control within the civilian government for the remainder of the war.

In fact, by 1937, given Japan's massive power in Manchuria and her growing threat to the rest of China, the Chinese communists and nationalists were forced to suspend their infighting and focus on fighting Japan. That year, the United States also began supplying some military assistance to China against the Japanese. In August, the country dispatched retired U.S. Army Air Corps General Claire Lee Chennault to China to advise Chaing Kai-Shek on organizing an air force resistance against the Japanese and to serve as an aviation trainer to the Chinese Air Force.

Japan, thus challenged, struck back with impunity. Her victories on the ground included the great city of Shanghai—the cultural mecca of China—and offered a glimpse of the brutal massacres for which the Japanese would become infamous. The Chinese lost over two hundred thousand men in that battle alone—half of the *total* number of souls lost by the United States during its four-year involvement in World War II. Between November of 1937 and January of 1938, the Japanese killed half a million Chinese. Overall, the Japanese ground war against China proved one of the most devastating slaughters of human life in history. In fact, from the Nanking Massacre in 1937 through the end of World War II, the Japanese would kill more than twenty million Chinese. Most of these casualties were inflicted on civilians. The Nanking Massacre itself became a massively publicized genocide which turned the United States and the West against Japan and led to the Allies giving aid to China during the first few years of the war. Following President Franklin Delano Roosevelt's declaration that the defense of China was vital to the defense of the United States, American "Lend-Lease" money began flowing to the country. The American president hoped to at least help feed starving Chinese soldiers in their less-than-effective operations against the more powerful and disciplined Japanese.

In addition, to establish at least a token military presence in the region, the United States recognized the "China-India-Burma" Theater of Operations, often referred to as the "CBI Theater." Under the command of Army General "Vinegar Joe" Stilwell, theater headquarters were established in Burma in early 1942, not long after the attack on Pearl Harbor. Most American and British firepower, however, remained concentrated in Europe, focusing on first defeating the Germans. That task was primarily assigned to the U.S. Army and British ground forces, while the U.S. Navy, U.S. Marines, and Royal Navy took on the brunt of the war in the Pacific. The Allied strategy involved having these forces attack from the east to keep Japan at bay in China and Southeast Asia. When Germany was on the ropes, the bulk of the U.S. Army could join the other branches in the Pacific for the impending invasion of Japan itself.

One of the notable Allied forces fighting in the region was the Chinese Expeditionary Force. Facing an increasingly unstable military situation, however, and with no substantial airfields in the CBI theatre, air support missions for this group had to be launched from the eastern Himalayas. These flights were necessary because the Japanese had shut down the Burma Road, which ran from Rangoon, Burma, along the Andaman Sea, into China, thereby cutting off the supply line for Chinese and Allied forces on the ground. Thus, air support became the only means of reinforcing those soldiers fighting the Japanese in China.

Most of the flights originated from bases in Assam, a state in Northeast India, to Kunming, a tropical city in Southwest China. Both the airbases in Assam and the City of Kunming were well west of the Japanese advance. It was a treacherous flight path that forced pilots to navigate the eastern end of the mammoth Himalayas, an area the pilots christened "the Hump." Because of the great height and size of the Himalayas, the erratic and violent wind shifts often caused the pilots to lose control of their aircraft, as the blinding weather conditions slammed them into the mountains' sides. Winds of two hundred miles per hour whipped out of nowhere. On occasion, the aircrafts' wings would ice over and the planes would drop like rocks, sending their crews to violent deaths below. A lack of reliable navigational charts and radio navigation aids made the pilots' situation even more precarious. In fact, from the Allies' first flight over the Hump in April of 1942 until the re-opening of the Burma Road, they lost six hundred aircraft and over sixteen hundred men along the route. Most of the dead were American.

This was the setup that greeted LeMay as he arrived in the Pacific theater in August of 1944. Japan controlled most of the populated area of China along her Pacific Coast. She was also far and away the dominant military power in Asia—between 1894 and 1931, the small island nation had fought wars against the two largest nations in the world (China and Russia) and beaten them both. In fact, in terms of impressive military victories since 1894, she had surpassed that of her better-known Axis partner Nazi Germany, which had suffered a humiliating defeat to the Allies in 1918. Excepting one debacle against the Russians in 1939 known as the battle of Khalkhin Gol, Japan had suffered no such defeats. She seemed unstoppable.

But she was also more brutal, ideological, less prone to any cooperation with the international community, and far more determined to fight to the last man than even the Germans LeMay had left behind. Both the Nazis and Japanese had committed inexcusable atrocities against humanity, but there had been one place where the Japanese sank even lower than their German counterparts, at least from a war-crimes standpoint. That was POW treatment. In contrast to the Japanese, the Nazis rendered relatively humane treatment to prisoners of war from France, Britain, and the United States. In these three instances, the Germans tended to follow the Geneva Convention protocol and even spared Jewish POWs wearing American, French, or British uniforms, although they employed unrestrained barbarism with Soviet POWs, killing some 3.3 million. But while the Nazis chose to exercise some caution with certain POWS, the Japanese barbarism towards POWs showed no restraint, regardless of the prisoners' nationality. Among the well-noted atrocities committed by Japanese forces against American and other captured Allied POWs were the notorious Bataan Death March in the Philippines in 1942; the torturing of American B-29 crews shot down over China; the Banka Island Massacre of 1942, in which the Japanese gunned down twenty-two Australian army nurses who were wearing Red Cross armbands, along with sixty Australian and British soldiers and crew members from two sunken ships; the Sandakan Death Marches—three forced marches on the Island of Borneo, resulting in the deaths of 2,345 mostly British and Australian soldiers; and the beheading and cannibalism of American pilots shot down over the Pacific. (Among American forces, word had gotten out of the extent of the brutal Japanese treatment of prisoners of war for at least a year before the battle for Iwo Jima had even commenced.)

Such incidents were a reflection of the brutality Japan inflicted across the region. The Dutch East Indies (now Indonesia) lost four million of its citizens at the hands of Imperial Japan by the end of World War II. French Indochina, which included the modern countries of Vietnam, Cambodia, and Laos, lost 1.5 million. The Philippines lost another million. By the time America ended the war with the deployment of the second atomic bomb, Japan had killed over twenty-six million people. In fact, when considering the widespread swath of pillage, murder, mayhem and torture all over eastern Asia, the Pacific and even the Indian Ocean regions, along with Japan's record of unbridled military victories in the twentieth century, a strong argument existed that Japan, and not Germany, was the most formidable, ruthless and dangerous nation in the world at the start of World War II. Such was the nature of the enemy LeMay now faced.

LeMay realized that, for the Allies to eventually strike Japan itself, the current flight route over the Himalayas was insufficient. Effective bombing raids against Japan would require a base of operations both closer to that country and easier to supply. Already devastated by the military licking Japan delivered, China had no internal airbases from which to launch strikes against the island nation. So LeMay searched for alternates. Such bases, at least for launching long-range bomber strikes, would become available in mid-1944 as U.S. forces captured the Marianas; once they secured Iwo Jima, they would finally have a spot that would allow their bombers to be protected by shorter-range fighter pilots. And so, on February 19, 1945, following three days of naval bombardment, the first of seventy thousand Marines had waded onto the island to face eighteen thousand Japanese soldiers dug into deep bunkers, craters, tunnels, and volcanic rock under orders to fight to the death. Once the Marines secured all of Iwo Jima, Jerry and his fellow fighter pilots could take off, join the bomber fleets already airborne from the Marianas, and attack targets over Japan itself.

CHAPTER 5

Hell Rains from the Skies

Iwo Jima
March 8, 1945

At 5:52 a.m., after twelve hours of darkness, the first ray of sunlight appeared above Jerry's foxhole. He had survived his first night on Iwo Jima. Dawn meant opportunity: to transform from hunted to hunter.

Against this sunny backdrop, Jerry and his fellow pilots were summoned and given their objective for the day. The Marines needed the pilots to fly close-air support on the island, which meant looping back over Iwo Jima after takeoff and flying down to dangerously low altitudes—ten to fifteen feet off the ground—while blasting Japanese ground troops with the six .50-caliber machine guns mounted in the wings of each plane. The Marines had already begun to map the entry points to many of the tunnels used by the Japanese to travel around the island and ambush Americans; the P-51s' fire from the sky would help root the enemy out.

The man in charge of the day's airstrike was Brigadier General Ernest M. "Mickey" Moore, who, like Curtis LeMay, had become a star in the U.S. Army Air Force. At thirty-seven, Moore was one of its youngest generals. With black, bushy eyebrows, a pearly white smile, and an Italian-looking pug nose, he bore a striking resemblance to the famous American actor, Humphrey Bogart. Even when Bogart—who had served in the Navy in World War I—suspended much of his movie-making to travel with the USO in 1943 and 1944 to war-torn sections of Africa and Italy, the comparisons with the young aviation officer persisted. While Bogart had been making movies, however, Moore was already living an adventurous life from which movies would later be made. In September of 1941, he won the Distinguished Flying Cross for leading a daring, long-range flight of nine B-17s from Pearl Harbor through Midway Atoll, Wake Island, Port Moresby, New Guinea, and Darwin, Australia, and then to Manila. With Moore in the cockpit, the Army Air Corps pushed the envelope with its planes, and especially its bombers, testing the efficacy of long-range bombing missions by flying over twelve thousand miles round trip. In fact, Moore's testing of B-17s over great distances in September of 1941 served as a building block for both the long-range bombing missions that LeMay and his fellow pilots would fly over Germany in 1943 and also the long-range bombing that would later be launched against Japan from the Mariana Islands.

Here in Iwo Jima, Moore had been given charge of Seventh Fighter Command, known as the "Sunsetters," which included Jerry and the rest of the Seventy-Eighth. The command was broken up into four different "fighter groups" of P-51s, with each group containing three fighter squadrons. At full deployment, each squadron was assigned thirty-seven planes, which meant the total number of P-51s on Iwo Jima reached approximately 444 planes at full strength. The groups, however, had staggered their arrival; the third group, known as the 506th, did not arrive on the island until April of 1945; the fourth group, called the 414th, would arrive in July of 1945. That meant, for now, Moore had only two fighter groups under his command: the Fifteenth—to which the Seventy-Eighth Fighter Squadron belonged—and the Twenty-First Fighter Group. Moore himself had flown the first fighter plane to land on Iwo Jima just fifteen days after the Marines stormed its beaches. But despite his status as a brilliant tactical aviator, the general lacked some of the superior fighter pilot skills shown by men like Jerry and had "pancaked" his plane upon landing at the base of Mount Suribachi (a "pancake landing" was an aviation term for when a plane made an emergency landing from a low altitude without first deploying the landing gear; the plane landed on its underside, or belly, which scraped against the surface of the earth, often running the risk of the plane flipping, disintegrating, or catching on fire).

This morning, Moore sent the Forty-Fifth Fighter Squadron into the air first, commanded by Major Gilmer L. "Buck" Snipes of Anderson, South Carolina. After takeoff, the Forty-Fifth flew over the ocean, then turned and started pouring a wall of .50-caliber lead into Japanese-held positions on the island. The angry fury from the powerful machine guns gave the Marines fighting on the ground an early-morning shot of adrenaline against the enemy.

Then came the Seventy-Eighth's turn.

For Jerry, just getting back into the bubble cockpit of the *Dorrie R* brought an electric, energetic feeling that washed away last night's nightmare. He listened to the seventeen-hundred-horsepower Rolls-Royce engine ignite and purr as he swung the plane around on the field and gave the "thumbs up" for takeoff. He pushed down on the Mustang's throttle and pulled back on the stick. The warbird rolled forward, picked up speed, and then lost contact with the soil of Iwo Jima. Under Jerry's skilled hands, she climbed into the sky and crossed out over the ocean.

Exhilaration overcame the young pilot. Here in the air—like all fighter pilots—he felt free. He swung out over the Pacific, then put the plane in a bank, turning in a large loop to head back to the island. As he closed back in on Iwo Jima, he felt a rush of adrenaline—he was about to engage in combat for the first time.

In the pilots' pre-flight briefing, they'd been told the Marines had fired yellow smoke grenades on target areas. Jerry and his companions' job was to find the smoke bombs and blast the living hell out of wherever the Japanese were hiding—and hopefully avoid getting shot down in the process.

Jerry brought the Mustang down low, almost as if he wanted to caress the top of the waves. He could see the whitecaps breaking as they rolled onto the beach below him. The plane roared back over the island. The first cloud of yellow smoke rose in a plume on the other side of the enemy lines.

He drew a bead on the source of the smoke, pushed the stick down and, flying right at the base of the smoke plume, let the .50-calibers rip off six flying streams of bullets directly at the target. The bullets tore up the ground in front of the plane, obliterating everything in their path. He had not seen any Japanese; they were likely hiding in the cave just below the surface. But nothing on the surface anywhere close to those bullets could have survived.

When he finally landed that day, back at Iwo Jima, it hit him: all the training he had done in the air, all the practice crisscrossing maneuvers and simulated dogfights, all the painful loss of his friends who had died alongside him, had brought him to this moment. Jerry Yellin had officially entered the war. There was no turning back. From now on, he had only two options: survival or death.

Over the next few days that followed, the pilots of the Fifteenth Fighter Group continued to pound ground targets all over Iwo Jima. Jerry himself flew mission after mission, strafing Japanese positions with machine-gun fire and hitting the Japanese with fifty-pound bombs.

Before, the Marines' only air support had been from U.S. Navy planes flying off escort carriers. These planes had dropped napalm— a propellant used in warfare, designed to burn people and things— from altitudes no lower than fifteen hundred feet. The Navy had been unable to maintain this air support, however, because of kamikaze attacks being flown into American ships by Japanese pilots. In addition, shifting wind conditions meant the napalm dropped from Navy planes at higher altitudes often proved unreliable in reaching its intended target. Acid spray from a stray U.S. Navy napalm would sometimes burn through a Marine's clothing and flesh, leaving the victim screaming and twisting in pain. But with the arrival of the Fifteenth Fighter Group, the P-51s now gave the Marines a more effective brand of close-air support. Because the attacks could be launched from a lower altitude, accidental friendly fire from American aircraft would be drastically reduced.

There was, however, a major problem. The Mustangs had ultimately come to launch long-range missions against Japan, not provide close-air support for the Marines. To that end, they'd been equipped with .50-caliber bullets instead of napalm, which rendered them far less effective in this instance. The Japanese had dug themselves so deep into holes and craters on the island that the best way to root them out was with smoke and fire. So the Fifteenth Fighter Group, working with Marine and Army explosive ordinance personnel, began building their own napalm bombs to use against the Japanese.

The results were devastatingly effective. Soon, the P-51s were raining napalm all over the island, turning large parts of it into a flaming inferno in the midst of the ocean. By the close of March 15, the Mustangs had flown their last close-air support on Iwo Jima. The remaining Japanese had retreated so deep underground that the Marines would have to go in and flush them out.

With their role on Iwo Jima winding down, Jerry and his fellow pilots felt anxious to commence the real reason they'd been brought to Iwo Jima: long-range flights to Japan. They were still waiting, however, for the rest of the Seventh Fighter Command to arrive. The Twenty-First would come soon; the 506th was farther behind.

One of the main holdups in their arrival was expanding a second airfield and completing a third on the island from which the Twenty-First and 506th could operate. The Japanese had originally begun work on the third airfield but never completed it, in part because of the repeated attacks from the U.S. military. The job of finishing the third airfield now fell to the Army engineers and U.S. Navy Seabees—in particular, the 133rd Navy Construction Battalion or "133 NCB." Despite the fact that they were trained as engineers, the Seabees of the 133rd were attached to the Fourth Marines and, along with them and the Fifth Marine Amphibious Corps, had been part of the first wave of troops to land on Iwo Jima's beaches. Before they ever distinguished themselves as engineers on Iwo Jima, they distinguished themselves in combat.

Not only did the Seabees offload supplies reaching the beachhead, but, armed with Browning Automatic Rifles and .30-caliber machine guns, they provided beach security teams that engaged the Japanese with active fire. Of the 790 Seabees who hit the beaches with the Marines on D-Day in Iwo Jima, forty were killed in action, 156 were wounded, two were declared missing and never found, and forty-eight were evacuated for sickness. The 133rd NCBs suffered 370 casualties, more than forty percent of the 790 men who landed, which totaled the highest percentage of casualties as part of a single battle in Seabee history.

Despite all that, the 133rd NCBs were the only unit in the first wave that did not receive the Presidential Unit Citation. But thanks to the NCBs' bravery in storming the beaches on February 19, 1945, military transport planes soon began flying into and out of South Field, resupplying the Marines on the ground and evacuating wounded Marines back to hospitals in the Marianas. With South Field operational, the Seabees began work on the 5,225-foot airstrip which had been constructed by the Japanese at Central Field, and which would eventually house the Twenty-First.

Meanwhile, as the Seabees labored, the American pilots on Iwo Jima had another mission to complete as they worked to clear any impediments to attacks on the Japanese homeland. The Marines and

Navy needed their help securing another crucial target: Chichi Jima, an island one hundred fifty miles to the north.

CHAPTER 6

The Chichi Jima Problem: The Last Impediment for the Fighters

Chichi Jima, also a part of the Bonin Islands, had grown into a full-fledged military obstacle for U.S. forces operating in the Pacific theater. The Japanese placed a high value on Chichi Jima, viewing it as a major stronghold and part of the final defense to the homeland. According to historian Chester Hearn in *Sorties into Hell: The Hidden War on Chichi Jima,* "To bolster morale, Emperor Hirohito sent his own palace guard of antiaircraft gunners to the island, because, in the opinion of his advisors, they were the best antiaircraft units in the empire." In addition, the Japanese were constantly enlarging and rebuilding their military airstrip on the island, which, if completed, could pose a significant problem to the American conquest of Iwo Jima. Each time the Americans launched an airstrike on Chichi Jima—mainly by U.S. Navy warplanes off aircraft carriers operating in the area—the Japanese started rebuilding the airstrip. Thus, the airstrip had to be attacked constantly to try to keep Japanese military aircraft at bay. The island also housed a major Japanese radio facility which boosted the Imperial Navy's communication with its ships and bases deep in the Pacific and intercepted messages from the

American fleet. All this posed a serious threat to the U.S. Navy and the American long-range bombers, which had already started attacking Japan without much-needed fighter escort.

Conquering Chichi Jima, however, was a taller order than even securing Iwo Jima. The latter, with the exception of the 560-foot-high Mount Suribachi, was primarily flat, which helped from a topographical standpoint. By contrast, the high, mountainous geography of Chichi Jima, crawling with at least twenty-five thousand Japanese troops, presented more of a challenge. American intelligence also assumed that most of the Japanese 109th Infantry Division was still stationed there (though that assumption turned out to be wrong). At one point, the U.S. Navy had devised a plan to capture the island, but when reality set in—that the steep topography and heavy gun bombardments on Chichi Jima would exact too heavy a price—the Navy opted for an alternate strategy that would involve multiple air strikes from carrier-based aircraft. In fact, U.S. Navy aviators had been targeting Chichi Jima long before Army fighter pilots even arrived on Iwo Jima. But while the Navy had succeeded in destroying the Japanese fighter planes on Chichi Jima, the island's radio stations continued to broadcast to Japanese forces in the Pacific.

The consequences, meanwhile, of getting shot down flying over or around Chichi Jima were enough to make even the bravest man's skin crawl. More than one of Jerry's brothers in arms had discovered this the hard way. On one Navy mission, the pilots and crew of four dive bombers, known as Avengers, had been ordered to attack a radio tower transmitter on the top of Mount Yoake on Chichi Jima. The Avenger was the Navy's largest carrier-based attack bomber; each plane carried four five-hundred-pound bombs. One by one, just after sunrise, each plane had launched off the deck of the *San Jacinto* into the rising sun. Down below, the rolling Pacific reflected a mix of the sun's rays and the light blue morning sky as the four-plane formation reached the shoreline of Chichi Jima. Based on the spectacular colors alone, one could almost forget the ferocity of war lurked so near.

The squadron commander, Navy Lieutenant Don Melvin, peeled off first and put his Avenger into a dive, zeroing in on the transmission station. But the American planes had been spotted by the Japanese, whose antiaircraft battalion responded. As tracers flew up from the ground, exploding all around him, Melvin kept his plane in attack mode, and, with bullets whizzing by his cockpit, released the plane's bombs toward the target before pulling out of the dive. Moments later, the other pilots in the squadron saw multiple explosions and an eruption of fire coming from the buildings surrounding the tower. From the air, it appeared that the first bombing run had caused damage, but the tower remained standing.

The next Avenger in the attack line, piloted by a young naval officer from Connecticut named George Herbert Walker Bush, followed into the flight leader's original path. With the map of the target strapped to his knee, he steered the plane into a steep, thirty-five-degree dive headed straight towards the tower.

Suddenly, a powerful burst of antiaircraft fire rocked the plane. Bush responded, executing an evasive maneuver by rolling the dive-bomber over and aiming the nose at the targeted tower. Now the plane was flying at the tower from an inverted position. Rapid pressure changes from the sudden loss of altitude caused intense pain in the pilot's eardrums, prompting him to shout at the top of his lungs to try and relieve the sharp, knifing sensation jabbing the inside of his ears. Somehow, he managed to right the plane. Checking his altimeter, the pilot bore down on his target. A surreal adrenaline saturated his body, and he opened the bomb bay doors and toggled the bomb-release switch.

Just as he released two five-hundred-pound bombs, another powerful antiaircraft burst exploded off his wing. Black splotches of antiaircraft gunfire appeared around the cockpit, which filled with smoke as more fire flamed across the crease of the wing and edged towards the fuel tanks. Despite his plane being hit, Bush stayed with the dive, determined to carry out his mission. He honed in on the target, dropped two more five-hundred-pound bombs, pulled up, pulled away, and banked the crippled plane off to the east towards the Pacific. Once over water, Bush leveled the aircraft at a few hundred feet above the surface. But he couldn't keep the plane in the air much longer. He ordered his crew members to bail out, then banked right to try and take the streaming flames off the door near his gunnery officer's station.

The aircraft lost altitude, morphing into an out-of-control metal fireball. Bush had no choice but to jump. He tried bailing out, but a wind gust slammed him head-first into the plane's tail section, nearly knocking him unconscious. Somehow, his parachute deployed, and in a moment of eerie silence, he hung in the wind—the island behind him, the ocean below. The water grew closer and closer, and a moment later, he splashed down into the Pacific, alive but bleeding from his head.

His crew members were not so fortunate. One's parachute did not deploy, and the hard fall into the water killed him on impact. The second never escaped from the fuselage of the falling plane and died as the Avenger plunged into the Pacific and sunk below the surface.

Bush, though still alive, faced a less than optimistic predicament himself. Battling strong currents as his blood gushed into the sea, he became a floating target for both Japanese naval boats and vicious sharks in the water. Yet he managed to deploy his life raft and pulled himself up into it even as Japanese boats sped toward him.

A sound from above brought a twist of fate. It came from U.S. Navy planes, which suddenly buzzed the skies overhead. Soon machine-gun fire cracked the air, with bullets furiously slashing and spraying the water all around Bush as the planes poured .50-caliber rounds at the attacking Japanese boats, driving them back from the pilot. Bush was eventually rescued after three hours at sea, disoriented, weeping, vomiting, and still bleeding from the head. Of the nine squadron members shot down that morning, Bush was the only one fortunate enough to escape capture at Chichi Jima. Every other

American airman except one was executed by the Japanese. Some were even cannibalized; Japanese military officials ordered their doctors to cut out the livers of some of the pilots' bodies, and the United States later discovered senior Japanese army officers hosted a Sake party for their Navy counterparts where the livers of American POWs were served as an appetizer. The Japanese Navy officers reciprocated by hosting a party where they butchered and served their own American POWs. These atrocities, uncovered in late 1945, became known as the "Chichi Jima Incident."[1]

Though this extent of Japanese barbarism against American POWs had yet to be fully exposed as Jerry and his peers prepared to write their own stories above Chichi Jima, rumors flew among American pilots that a shoot-down over any Japanese enclave—especially Chichi Jima—would lead to Japanese cannibalism. Stories circled that the Japanese amputated a leg from still-living American pilots and ate the limb piecemeal before amputating the other leg and eating it too. Unfortunately, the rumors were true.

But they also gave the U.S. pilots extra motivation. Attacking Chichi Jima was an absolute necessity on a tactical level, but, in addition, it offered the American pilots a chance at revenge for what the Japanese had done to their peers.

And the payback from the Seventh Fighter Wing would start on the morning of March 11, 1945.

CHAPTER 7

Hitting Chichi Jima

March 11, 1945

With the Marines continuing to gain the upper hand against the isolated but still dangerous Japanese forces on Iwo Jima, Jerry and the other squadron pilots of the Seventy-Eighth emerged from their foxholes on the morning of March 11 to receive orders that had come down from Colonel Jim Beckwith, commanding officer of the Fifteenth Fighter Group. Their group was told they'd continue pressing aerial attacks against the Japanese on Iwo Jima. Seventeen Mustangs from the Forty-Seventh Fighter Squadron, meanwhile, would be assigned the first strike against Chichi Jima. Colonel Beckwith, as group commander, and Brigadier General Moore, as commander over the entire Seventh Wing, would accompany the men of the Forty-Seventh on the attack.

At nine a.m., the pilots of the Forty-Seventh began to lift off one by one from Iwo Jima. Flying a holding pattern until all seventeen planes were in the sky, the "Dogpounders," the nickname they had adopted, organized into the "four finger" formations for the 150-mile flight north. Moore, flying under the code name "Chieftan One," stayed outside the formation as the seventeenth pilot.

Seventy-five miles out, they passed a U.S. Navy PBY Catalina, known as a "seaplane," capable of landing in the sea and often used in search-and-rescue operations. The Catalina patrolled the ocean, tasked with picking up any Mustang pilot who might have to bail out of his aircraft either on the approach to Chichi Jima or the return flight. As an additional precaution, the Navy had positioned at least one destroyer off the island for potential rescue operations.

The pilots were now sixty miles out. As the minutes passed, tension rose inside the cockpit of each P-51. It was one thing to provide close-air support for the Marines against Japanese ground troops on Iwo Jima. On Chichi Jima, however, the Japanese boasted dangerous antiaircraft defenses—ones that had already brought torture and death to many American pilots.

Soon, twenty-five-year-old Captain Ray L. Obenshain Jr., flying as Blue Flight leader, looked off to the right of his cockpit and saw the mountainous contour of Chichi Jima rising from the sea. Obenshain radioed his sighting to the sixteen other planes.

The pilots exchanged thumbs up. As Moore broke off into a holding pattern about one mile southwest of the Americans' principal target, Colonel Beckwith, flying lead in Red Flight, led the rest of the group in a low pass across the water, just southeast of the airfield. This position would allow the Mustangs to commence their aerial assault from the direction of the rising sun, giving them a blinding advantage against the Japanese antiaircraft gunners that would soon be firing into the skies.

Turning his plane back to the northwest, Beckwith pushed down on his throttle and nosed the Mustang down.

The airfield was a single-strip, dirt-surfaced runway sitting at the top of a hill and had already been bombed frequently by high-flying Americans B-24s out of Guam. In fact, the pattern had been the same for many months: the Americans would bomb the airfield, then the Japanese would repair it.

On this mission—just as Beckwith's intelligence briefings had reported—the Japanese had again graded the runway. Four Japanese warplanes sat there, with three of the four appearing operational. Those planes would need to be taken out before they could get airborne and cause trouble. Leading his Red Flight down to four thousand feet, Beckwith released two five-hundred-pound bombs on the airstrip, then pulled out and headed offshore into a holding pattern as antiaircraft fire and black smoke began to rise from the island.

Moore, flying an observation pattern a mile out, watched as Beckwith's men, following in tight formation, pressed their attack on the airfield with surgical precision, flying through Japanese flack to drop seven more bombs and strafe the aircraft at the end of the runway.

As the Red, Blue, and Green Flights rained hell on the airfield, the Yellow Flight turned its fury to the harbor. With Captain John Piper leading, the four Mustangs soared over Shiomi Point, taking aim at sixteen smaller seagoing vessels moored in the harbor. The Yellow Flight unleashed a salvo of bombs, some finding their targets. The group pulled up, circled again, and took aim at the seaplane base, which had been added by the Imperial Japanese Navy at the start of the war for reconnaissance missions against the U.S. Navy. In fact, the seaplane base had been just as much of a pain to the American fleet and American aircraft as the ground-based airstrip had been. Now, the Mustangs' .50-caliber bullets sent water spraying into the sky and disabled several of the Japanese seaplanes from taking off.

Satisfied with the damage inflicted, Beckwith set a course for a brief, thirty-one-minute flight to the nearby island of Haha Jima, also known to be a Japanese stronghold. There was no point in *not* blasting the Japanese some more on the way back to Iwo Jima, he'd decided. The Mustangs had already dropped their bombs, so this time, they stayed with .50-caliber bullets, unleashing several hundred rounds on Haha Jima before finally turning back to Iwo Jima.

Overall, Beckwith and Moore were pleased that the air assault considered a prelude to attacking Japan had gone off without a single scratch to any American plane. Everybody knew, however, that luck would eventually turn. In war, bloodshed was unavoidable, even for the victors. But for now, they appreciated a victory gained without the loss of American pilots' lives.

Over the next few days in March, the three squadrons of the Fifteenth Fighter Group on Iwo Jima established a rotation. One hit Chichi Jima while the second provided close-air support for the Marines. The third spent a maintenance day on the ground, preparing to fly in the rotation the next day. The exception was Beckwith, who, like the Green Mountain Boys of his Vermont heritage, could not resist a golden chance to take the fight to the enemy. Beckwith personally flew combat missions to Chichi Jima for three consecutive days.

On that third day—March 13, 1945—Jerry's turn to attack Chichi Jima arrived. So far, his tour in the Pacific had been productive—so much so that, since arriving on Iwo Jima, he'd already been promoted to captain. He and his squadron mates had been anxious to give Chichi Jima a taste of what the "Bushmasters" (the nickname for the Seventy-Eighth) could deliver; in addition, the chance to go into battle with his mentor, Jim Tapp, who would later go down in history as one of the Air Force's greatest aces, sent an extra thrill coursing through Jerry's veins.

The Seventy-Eighth's mission this time followed the pattern their predecessors had established. Jerry and his squadron mates piloted their crafts in formation to Chichi Jima, and, once there, Jerry slid his Mustang down to four thousand feet, dropped two five-hundred-pound bombs, pulled out, re-positioned, and pummeled the seaplane base. It was yet another "maintenance strike" against Chichi Jima, all part of a constant effort to keep the enemy at bay. Altogether, the Mustangs would fly almost 140 missions against the Japanese strongholds on Chichi Jima and Haha Jima, striking daily to make way for the American fleet to operate without detection and increase protection for American B-29s on the eighteen-hundred-mile round-trip bombing runs from the Mariana Islands to Japan.

But the Japanese were far from finished.

CHAPTER 8

In the Mind of the Enemy

March 24, 1945

During the American Civil War, soldiers of the Confederate Army would employ a tactic in battle that sent shivers up the spines of young Union troops the first time they encountered it.

Charging across the field in a massive human wave, brandishing bayonets that flashed in the bright sun, the gray-clad, wild-eyed rebels, while firing rifles, unleashed in unison a blood-curdling scream. The scream became known as the "rebel yell" and ignited terror in anyone facing the onslaught. According to the great Civil War historian Shelby Foote, one Union soldier said, "[I]f you claim you heard it and weren't scared, that means you never heard it."

Here in the Pacific theater, the Japanese had employed their own version of mass psychological intimidation on a battlefield, and American forces had a name for the Japanese tactic. They called it "Banzai," and both Japanese fighter pilots and Japanese soldiers embraced the concept. While Banzai did not consist of vocal screaming by Japanese troops, it proved, in some ways, even more fearful and dangerous. It was the idea that killing oneself for the glory of the emperor

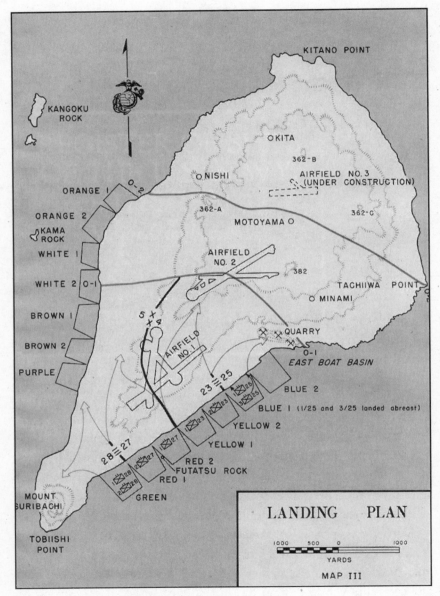

This map shows the different airfield locations on Iwo Jima.

was more illustrious than surrender. To carry out this ideological conviction, the soldiers would rush in waves at an opposing army, running across a field brandishing bayonets and exposing themselves to enemy fire. One of the largest such attacks had come in the battle of Saipan less than a year before Jerry arrived on Iwo Jima: over forty-three hundred Japanese troops had charged the American lines in a last-ditch suicide charge. These Banzai tactics erupted towards the end of a battle, and only when Japanese forces had clearly lost. To surrender, they felt, was cowardice.

But for the American pilots on Iwo Jima, it appeared by March 24 that the danger of such an attack was slim to none. The Marines had made excellent progress chasing the Japanese from the island; in fact, on March 15, 1945, the Mustangs had been told to stand down in flying close-air support for the Marines, who were in the last stages of a mop-up operation. The final few skirmishes were so tightly quartered that even the P-51s would pose too much of a friendly-fire hazard to the Marines. By the following day, Iwo Jima was declared "secure" from serious Japanese threat on the island. Iwo Jima, with its precious airfields, was now poised to give the Army Air Force enhanced striking capability against Japan.

Such victory had come at a high price. Between the beginning of the invasion of Iwo Jima on February 19, 1945, and the time the island was declared secure on March 16, 4,189 Marines had been killed and 19,938 wounded. The U.S. death toll on Iwo Jima eventually climbed to over 6,000 killed—primarily Marines—and nearly 26,000 wounded. Japanese defenders, meanwhile, had originally numbered about 21,000, of which only 1,083 survived.

The Fifteenth Fighter Group, meanwhile, had been reinforced by the Twenty-First Fighter Group, commanded by Colonel Ken Powell. Ground elements of the Twenty-First had begun arriving by the end of February, but the P-51s from the Twenty-First did not reach Iwo Jima until March 15.

As additional air units arrived on Iwo Jima in preparation for a great April air raid against Japan, the new groups set up base on airstrips other than the one originally occupied by Jerry and the men of the Fifteenth. Jerry's field, the one closest to Mount Suribachi, was known as Airfield No. 1, or South Field. The Twenty-First Fighter Group—consisting of the Forty-Sixth, Seventy-Second, and 531st fighter squadrons—began using the airfield in the center of the island, known as Airfield No. 2, or Central Field. Airfield No. 3, or North Field, was the last airfield to be constructed and would not be available until May 11, 1945.

Meanwhile, with victory on the ground in sight and more aircraft flying into Iwo Jima each day in preparation for massive air assaults over Japan, American naval forces had begun withdrawing from Iwo Jima, their skills needed elsewhere. The Marines who'd been part of the original invasion force were also moving on; they were being replaced by the 147th Infantry Regiment of the U.S. Army. The change showed the stability the Americans had achieved on the island. The P-51 pilots, for their part, could feel secure knowing Iwo Jima itself was secure. All the Japanese were gone from the island.

Or so they thought.

CHAPTER 9

Prelude to a Massacre

March 25, 1945

March 25, 1945, arrived as a peaceful Sunday on Iwo Jima. Jerry and the other Americans there were enjoying a brief—if perhaps eerie—respite from the bloodiness of battle. Back in the United States, millions of Americans prepared to attend worship services to pray for husbands and sons overseas. So far, by the grace of God, the Fifteenth had lost only one flyer since arriving on Iwo Jima: First Lieutenant Beaver Ashley Kinsel of the Forty-Fifth Fighter Squadron. Kinsel, an experienced combat pilot despite his youth, had disappeared in the clouds on routine combat air patrol not far off Iwo Jima earlier that month. Nobody knew what had happened. Fatigue or pilot error were possibilities, but given Kinsel's reputation as one of the best young pilots in the Forty-Fifth, it was probably a mechanical failure that had cost him his life. His comrades never found his plane. The twenty-three-year-old pilot's death served up a cold reminder to them: no one could take anything for granted.

Today, however, offered a semblance of normalcy. Conditions had improved marginally for Jerry since his arrival. The fighter pilots were now living in tents; there was no longer a need to sleep in smelly foxholes, worry about mortars flying into the camp, or fear the Japanese materializing from nowhere. The nights themselves were quieter now, for the constant sounds of war had subsided. Except for the sound of a P-61 taking off or landing on night patrol, there was actually a chance for sweet sleep.

The newly arrived men of the Twenty-First, however, had not seen the combat the men of the Fifteenth had. While members of the Fifteenth considered this a relative lull, the new pilots on the island, shocked by what they saw, were still trying to adjust. Captain Howard Russell of the Seventy-Second Fighter Squadron wrote in his ongoing diary,

> The destruction, filth, and total lack of vegetation were unbelievable. Our camp was set up just west and downhill from the middle airstrip and consisted of pyramidal tents, row on row, which were to be considered luxurious compared to our later combat quarters. Our operations tent on the airfield was next to the remains of a concrete structure which was the surface building of a three to four level cave dwelling reportedly used by the Japanese as a hospital. The Marines had done a nice job of sealing it and we felt confident that any Japs inside were there to stay....
>
> Sleep was hard coming and each night skirmishes with the enemy not far north of our camp made us keep one eye and both ears open. Food was "C" ration heated in a trash can of water, and sometimes "K" ration was issued. The Marines had better food and we often bartered for their one gallon cans of good stuff.

Russell's commander, Colonel Ken Powell, also wrote about his first night on the island:

A young Navy officer approached me. He was one of my YMCA camp boys from Washington State and had heard I was on Iwo. He invited me to join him for dinner and I didn't waste any time dropping my mess kit. He took me to his screened mess tent, with mess attendants, where I was served steak and all the trimmings. He was a lieutenant in charge of a couple of PBYs and I was a colonel with 100 fighter planes eating from a mess kit while sitting on a crate. The Navy really lived right.

Despite the shuttling of troops and the appearance of serenity, Paul Schurr and his 531st Squadron tent mates had an uneasy feeling and spent the day digging a foxhole, using the material to fill sandbags which were placed around their tent and the top of the hole.

Schurr and John Galbraith bartered with departing Marines for a Garand rifle, a Carbine and several belts of ammo. The pilots had arrived on Iwo armed only with .45 caliber pistols. They spent the evening cleaning their new arsenal by lantern light.

Perhaps Schurr and Galbraith knew something in their guts nobody else did.

On the evening of March 25, one of their peers in the Twenty-First Fighter Group, Captain Harry Crim, entered his tent and decided to turn in early. The next day, the 531st would be in the skies, ready to strike Japanese targets and provide a supplemental boost to the men of the Fifteenth Fighter Group. Like Jim Tapp, Crim was one of the Army's top aces. In a nearby tent, under a three-quarters moon that brought a faint glow to the war-torn island, Powell had also gone to bed ahead of the big day for the Twenty-First. As the moon climbed higher in the sky, the pilots of two fighter groups started to fall asleep.

Meanwhile, all through the day and night, men from both fighter groups flew round-the-clock air patrols around the island. The patrols involved at least eight planes airborne at any given time, watching for Japanese aircraft or ships. They generally took off just before sundown in two-hour increments and flew patrols in four-hour shifts throughout the night. In the evenings, many of the patrols were flown by squadrons of P-61 "Night Fighters": twin-engine, twin-tailed Black Widow aircraft. Unlike the faster, more maneuverable P-51s, the P-61s, because of their design, rarely engaged in dogfights but proved best at flying long-range reconnaissance missions and intercepting the Japanese Mitsubishi G4M bombers, or the "Betty," as the American pilots called the principal land-based bomber used by the Japanese Navy in World War II. The Betty possessed great range for a bomber because its lighter weight allowed it to fly farther to strike its targets, and it could also carry more bombs. If the Betty was able to slip through fighter coverage, especially at night, and deliver its payload, it could be devastating.

But there was a drawback as well. By sacrificing the weight of the aircraft to achieve greater speed and distance, the Betty was very thin on protective armament. In contrast to the more heavily armored American bombers, which often could take enemy machine-gun fire and limp back to base, the Bettys did not enjoy that luxury. They also did not have self-sealing fuel tanks, a newer technology with multiple layers of rubber designed to prevent fuel leaks. With the slightest machine-gun fire, the Bettys often burst into flames. To be effective, the Betty had to sneak in and launch its bombs high above its target. It needed fighter protection, which often took the form of the much-heralded Mitsubishi AM-6 fighter aircraft, colloquially known as the Japanese "Zero." The Japanese often flew the Bettys on night missions, theorizing that the darkness made them harder for American fighters to spot. To combat the Bettys' night missions, the Army countered with the American P-61 "Black Widows," the first combat aircraft in the world designed to use radar, thereby allowing them to "see" enemy aircraft, even at night. In fact, the P-61s often proved an effective deterrent to the Betty—though the P-61s rarely engaged them, the Betty would often turn tail and run if it spotted one. Multiple instances were recorded in which the Betty, after seeing a Black Widow, dropped all its bombs in the ocean to lighten its load and increase speed before zooming as fast as it could out of the area. Even so, the men flying air patrol exercised a healthy concern about the threat the Betty posed.

Under the command of Captain Ernest Thomas, the first Black Widow had taken off from Iwo Jima's Central Field at dusk on March 25. Although Iwo Jima was located just south of the twenty-fifth parallel, putting it on a latitudinal line almost equal with Key Largo, Florida, and the Gulf of Mexico, the night was chilly for the tropics. Inside the cockpit, it felt even colder. "We had not brought the proper clothing," Thomas noted in his log. "When flying, it was worse. The aircraft heaters didn't work and there were no parts available. We had no warm flight clothing and no gloves. It was often below freezing when flying at high altitudes. We usually patrolled at 15,000 to 18,000 feet."

At 10:15 p.m., the round, green radar screen at ground control on Iwo Jima swept the skies around the island and noted no activity except the eight P-61s on combat air patrol.

Within fifteen minutes, the status changed. Ground radar on Iwo Jima detected invaders from the north. In seconds, air raid sirens blared across the island. Searchlights crisscrossed the skies. Antiaircraft gunners rushed to theirs stations. The Americans on Iwo Jima hunkered down for a potential onslaught of bombs.

Thomas, patrolling over three miles above the ocean, had been in the air for more than four hours and was about to bring his plane back into Central Field. His radar officer, however, had already spotted the inbound enemy aircraft. That was quickly followed by a radio call from ground control confirming the news.

Thomas turned the Black Widow and set it on an intercept course, but, since he was at the end of his scheduled patrol, the plane's fuel was perilously low. Ground control at Airfield No. 1 was about to order him back to base, but before they issued the command, another enemy entity appeared on the ground radar. A Betty bomber had swung wide around the island—at first outside of radar range—and was now headed north, on course for a bombing run over Iwo Jima. The command at ground control now faced a dilemma: they could either bring Thomas back in because of low fuel and scramble additional Black Widows to go out and challenge the newly discovered bomber, or they could send Thomas after the Betty and gamble that his fuel wouldn't run out. If they opted for the first method, the Betty could deliver its massive bombing load before more Black Widows managed to get airborne.

The call fell to Lieutenant Colonel Jimmy Alford, group commander of the Black Widows. He knew the crew onboard Thomas's aircraft was one of his most experienced; it included, along with Thomas, radar officer John Acre and gunner Corporal Jesse Tew. Alford wanted those guys in the fight. He decided to push the plane a little harder.

"Abort landing," Alford ordered. "Vector to incoming bogey. Take him out."

On board the Black Widow, a surge of adrenaline rushed through the cold cockpit. Thomas set his Black Widow on an intercept vector with the approaching Betty. The next few minutes would determine whether he and his crew lived or died.

Tension mounted in the plane as Thomas kept his bird flying in an intercept vector. Staring into the black skies, Thomas strained to find the enemy plane silhouetted somewhere in the moonlight.

"Radar contact, captain!" Acre announced as he spotted the enemy plane's blip on the Black Widow's radar.

Fifteen thousand feet above the dark waters of the Pacific, the men kept scouring the heavens.

"There!" Tew observed the Betty's outline in the moonlight. "Down below."

Thomas looked down and put the plane into a dive. But because they had spotted the enemy almost directly below them, the Black Widow overshot its position as the Japanese craft initiated an evasive maneuver and climbed steeply up to nineteen thousand feet. The planes had effectively switched positions, with Thomas and his crew losing the enemy in the stars overhead.

Thomas pulled back on the yoke, putting the P-61 into a climb. He would find the Betty or run out of fuel trying.

Twice more, the P-61 located and lost the Japanese bomber as the deadly game of cat-and-mouse continued. Finding the enemy on radar was one thing, but getting a visual sighting in the inky black skies, and then pulling close enough for a decent shot, was quite another.

Meanwhile, the Betty closed in on Iwo Jima, now flying above the range of the Americans' antiaircraft batteries on the island. At this rate, it would cross the island, drop its bombs, and disappear into the night.

The P-61 was running out of time—and fuel. One certainty dominated each passing moment: the imminence of death, whether it be for the crew of the P-61, those onboard the Betty, or American pilots on the ground on Iwo Jima, defenseless against the Betty's powerful bombs.

"Look! Up there!" Thomas called. "There he is again."

The Betty had once more appeared in the moonlight. The Black Widow climbed up and moved in behind the bomber at an even altitude. The Betty was cruising towards Iwo Jima at 155 miles per hour.

Thomas pushed the throttle forward to increase air speed. It wasn't clear yet if the Americans had been spotted by the Betty. So far, the Japanese craft had not taken evasive action.

"One thousand feet downrange."

"Eight hundred feet."

Thomas wrapped his finger around the trigger of the .50-caliber machine gun and took aim at the Betty's left engine, mounted under the wing.

"Seven hundred feet."

"Six hundred feet."

Thomas squeezed the trigger, firing a short, quick burst from the plane's machine gun.

The Black Widow jumped, and a second later, the Betty's left engine burst into flames, illuminating the night sky.

Thomas pushed down on the yoke, diving just under the fuselage of the burning bomber to avoid a collision. The top of the Black Widow passed within feet of the enemy craft's underside. Thomas pulled his plane hard right, and, a second later, the P-61 reached clear airspace. Its crew watched the Betty transform into a falling comet, streaking through the black night to its watery grave in the Pacific.

One threat was gone.

But the Americans were still ninety-five miles from Iwo Jima, haunted by another unanswered question: would they be flying or swimming home?

A little over thirty minutes later, with its fuel gauges showing "empty" but the engines continuing to run, Thomas's P-61 touched down on Central Field. Bringing the plane to its station position at the end of the runway, Thomas received the good news: thanks to his crew's heroic work chasing down the Betty, and the work of his fellow pilot, Lieutenant Myrle McCumber of the 548th Night Fighter Squadron, the rest of the Japanese bombers had turned and fled. McCumber and his crew hit two Bettys and shot down a third that had closed within fifty miles of Iwo Jima, or just minutes away from the island. Because of the Night Fighters' efforts, Iwo Jima would be secure for the rest of the evening.

Or would it?

It was one thing to battle Japanese aircraft. At least they were visible on radar, even at night.

It was quite another to go to war against ghosts.

CHAPTER 10

Massacre of the Night Fighters

Field Headquarters—Twenty-First Fighter Group
Iwo Jima
March 26, 1945

Other than the near-miss with the Japanese Bettys, the night on the island had so far proved uneventful for the men of the Twenty-First Fighter Group. Newcomers Gailbraith and Schurr, however, were taking no chances—they made sure to keep their newly acquired rifles, courtesy of the U.S. Marine Corps, close at hand.

After the air raid sirens had subsided and the Night Fighters successfully hunted their men, silence again blanketed the dark night on the island. The first P-51s were scheduled to be in the air just twenty-two minutes after sunrise, slated for 5:32 that morning.

The three o'clock hour came and went peacefully.

The four o'clock hour arrived.

Suddenly, a mortar explosion rocked the night air, sending sharp shrapnel flying. One piece tore through Harry Crim's tent with such a powerful blast that it knocked him to the floor.

Something had gone horribly wrong.

It had to be the Japanese.

But where the hell had they come from?

Crim grabbed a .45-caliber pistol and rushed out into the darkness.

Across the way, the command tent, which housed Powell and several other senior officers, had collapsed from mortar fire. The Japanese were crawling all over the camp, their menacing silhouettes visible in the fading moonlight. An hour and a half before sunrise, the Twenty-First was under a surprise Banzai attack from Japanese who were not even supposed to be on the island. The Americans' crisis was compounded by the fact that most of the Marines had already pulled out. The few who remained and their replacements from the U.S. Army were clustered elsewhere on the island, currently unaware of the ambush.

Crim realized he needed more than a pistol. He ran back into the tent, grabbed a carbine, popped a magazine in it, and snatched several other magazines full of bullets. Crouching low, he sprinted across the camp and took cover behind a berm.

There. About 150 feet downrange. At least thirty armed Japanese soldiers had crawled into a large hole in the ground at the end of the camp.

Crim worked the bolt on the carbine and took aim. He pulled the trigger, and his shot pierced the air. He pulled the trigger again and again, raining .30-caliber bullets down on the enemy. Some slumped over.

Crim adjusted his aim and fired again. More Japanese fell. Others scrambled.

But they were far from finished.

■ ■ ■

At the tent occupied by Captain Jim Van Nada and six other officers of the Seventy-Second Fighter Squadron, a hand grenade exploding outside the flap entrance woke the pilots inside. Before they could get their bearings, the Japanese tossed a second grenade into the tent.

"Hit the deck!" someone shouted.

But the grenade landed under Van Nada's cot before he could react. The subsequent explosion sent shrapnel penetrating his left leg and knee joint.

Dazed, the pilots scrambled to find their .45-caliber pistols, determined to get outside. Three of the pilots, Lieutenants Canfield, Rogers, and Howard, rushed out of the tent. As Van Nada and his buddy, Lieutenant Bruner, started to step out, another grenade blast knocked them back inside. Van Nada fell backward, bleeding again.

Canfield, Rogers, and Howard, meanwhile, had exposed themselves to Japanese rifle fire by leaving the tent. An enemy bullet struck Howard. Canfield and Rogers also took bullets and stumbled back into the tent. Both writhed in agony for much of the night. Rogers died before it ended; Canfield passed away that morning. Of the three pilots who left the tent, only one, Howard, survived.

In fact, the scene outside the tent was a nightmare. With most of the Marines gone, the American pilots suddenly found themselves facing off against Japanese infantry in a mortal struggle of hand-to-hand combat. Bullets ripped through tents, tearing the canvas and whizzing by pilots' heads. Four more pilots, headed toward their aircraft to begin combat air patrol, were also ambushed and killed by the Japanese.

Even amid the chaos, it was abundantly clear an intelligence failure had led to the island mistakenly being declared secure on March 16. Hundreds of Japanese had remained hidden underground, burrowed in caves and subterranean labyrinths. Like ghosts rising from a graveyard, they crawled out of their holes by the dozens, brandishing their weapons in a last stand against the enemy and committing their bodies to suicide for the emperor. Around the camp, these desperate men huddled in craters, lobbing grenades into the Americans' tents. Yelling "Banzai," they leaped from cover and made suicidal charges towards the structures, brandishing bayonets and rifles.

The American pilots, for their part, weren't infantrymen, and they preferred fighting in the skies rather than on the ground. But they were determined to fight back as the Japanese made their last stand on Iwo Jima. All around the camp, the lightly armed airmen grouped together in tents to resist the Japanese. Most were carrying .45-caliber pistols; they faced a field army with rifles, bayonets, hand-grenades, and other explosives.

Among the grittily determined Americans was Crim. Seeing his commander's tent had been partially brought down by a grenade, he crouched low and ran through a wave of Japanese bullets, successfully reaching the tent to check on the group leader and his staff. "It was a hell of a mess," he described later in his diary. "They had all been hit by grenade fragments and there was blood all over. Ken Powell had been raked with shrapnel from ankle to waist and was bleeding profusely."

The northeastern corner of the camp, where Powell's tent was located, had been hit hard. In one tent, occupied by five pilots of the 531st squadron, the results were disastrous: two men, Lieutenants Woods and Mattill, were killed instantly by exploding hand grenades, while three others, Lieutenants Cheney, Wailes, and Miller, were badly wounded. The Japanese quick-stepped into the tent to established a command post. Off to the side, Cheney and Wailes were moaning in pain. This irritated the Japanese, who slit the officers' throats. Miller, the final member of the pilot quintet, feigned death for several hours.

Meanwhile, as the cacophony of rifle shots and men screaming in agony from bullets and shrapnel ripping into their bodies pierced the night air, Dr. George Hart, flight surgeon for the Forty-Sixth squadron, swung into action. Hart, a native of Lake Placid, New York, dashed through a slew of bullets to set up a temporary field hospital in a bulldozed depression. It was there Crim dragged Powell, who was still bleeding profusely. Dr. Hart started immediate emergency treatment on his wounds. With his commanding officer secure, Crim returned to the battle.

The Japanese had continued to attack pilots inside their tents by throwing grenades into the structures and firing into them. Many pilots lay bleeding and injured inside, requiring Crim and whoever he could find to conduct a tent-by-tent sweep as they tried to relocate injured pilots to the field hospital. He found helping hands in Major Sam Hudson, the commanding officer of the 531st Fighter Squadron, and Lieutenant Harry Koke. With Hudson in charge, all three men, bullets whizzing by their heads, checked each tent, working methodically and dodging shrapnel from mortars and grenades. "We operated as a team, two covering the tent while one raised a flap and looked in," Crim later wrote. "The wounded we found, we'd put on a blanket and drag back to Dr. Hart." They had their work cut out for them—a number of the men had already been shot or injured by shrapnel.

Fifteen to twenty minutes later, just as the trio reached the far side of the camp, a platoon of Japanese soldiers, who were hiding in three tents they'd taken over, opened fire. Crim and Hudson managed to dodge the sudden barrage of bullets, but Koke was hit. Despite this, he stayed with Crim and Hudson as long as he could as they moved on to investigate the larger tents, looking for comrades needing medical assistance. After checking several structures, however, Koke's blood loss required he get back to the field hospital for treatment before losing consciousness. Koke peeled off, while Hudson and Crim kept searching.

Once they were satisfied all the wounded had been evacuated to the field hospital, they went back on the offensive. Organizing an armed line with a third comrade, Technical Sergeant Philip Jean of Texas, from the 549th Night Fighter Squadron, they moved through the camp, shooting at the Japanese with their .45-caliber pistols. Even in the Army Air Force, those boys from Texas were good with guns.

During those early morning hours of March 26, 1945, Jean became an American hero. Operating a Browning Automatic rifle with the proficiency of a U.S. Marine, he squeezed off fifty rounds against the enemy, single-handedly killing up to eleven Japanese in the dark of the night, all while under fire himself. Though Jean would survive the night and even his deployment on Iwo Jima, he would never set foot on the soil of his beloved Texas again. He was later lost at sea, then declared missing in action, with his official date of death April 1, 1946. His body was never recovered, nor is there a grave for him. His memory, however, is today reflected in a solitary marker at the Tablets of the Missing in a Honolulu cemetery. He received a Purple Heart posthumously, but the failure to also recognize his heroism with a Silver Star remains a question mark, if not a travesty. Perhaps, if he had only lived longer, his deeds would not have faded so quickly in the annals of history.

And yet, that night, he struck back with fury, as did many of his fellow Americans. He was a fitting representative of the brave, intrepid, non-commissioned airmen who fought like ground warriors in the face of some of the most vicious fighters known to man.

Meanwhile, before reinforcement arrived from the Army, the handful of Marines still left behind and other enlisted men working as aircraft mechanics, gunners, and crews picked up pistols, carbines, and rifles and started taking the fight back to the Japanese. Approximately two hours after the ambush started, Captain Robert J. Munro of the nearby Fifth Marine Pioneer Battalion drove up with a handful of Marine engineers and a truck filled with ammo, including hand-grenades, rifles, and automatic weapons. The length of time it had taken them to arrive was understandable, albeit tragic. Just as they had done at Pearl Harbor, the Japanese had achieved the element of surprise. The Americans, having declared victory, had already reduced the internal security on the island, shifting their primary defenses from boots on the ground to radar and fighter aircraft. The troops who remained were scattered in other parts of the island, which contributed to the delay in first recognizing the emergency, then reacting in a timely manner.

The geography of the island hadn't helped, either. The tents housing the sleeping members of the Twenty-First Fighter Group and the newly arrived members of the 549th Night Fighter Squadron were set up on the north side of Airfield No. 2. At the time, Airfield No. 3 remained under construction by U.S. Navy Seabees and was still unoccupied. The construction, in fact, was proving to be an engineering challenge. Not only had the Seabees started it while the field was still in a war zone, but building runways long enough and strong enough to land a B-29 Superfortress on solidified lava and ash proved difficult. The initial portion of the work—to prepare the sub-grade for the landing strip—required the Seabees to bulldoze and then move about two hundred thousand cubic yards of rock and volcanic ash. The lava rock weighed around twelve hundred pounds per cubic yard. Overall, the Seabees moved about 240 million pounds of lava rock just to strip down the future runway and prepare it for the sub-grade of the landing field. The two runways already completed were nearly a mile in length, and most of the departing Marines, Army units, and others, including U.S. Navy Seabees, were camped either along the coastal region to the southeast of Airfield No. 1 or between the base of Mount Suribachi and the southwest end of Airfield No. 1. That meant most of the Army was over a mile away from the Twenty-First Fighter Group's camp and outside the immediate earshot of gunfire erupting there. Jerry and the men of the Seventy-Eighth Fighter Squadron, meanwhile, along with the other squadrons of the Fifteenth Fighter Group, were also camped well over a mile away from their counterparts of the Twenty-First.

But when the Marines finally did arrive to assist the Twenty-First, the momentum began shifting against the Japanese. Munro and his Marines started a tent-by-tent sweep of the north section of the camp, hunting the enemy. As the Marines pinned the Japanese down with rifle fire, arriving U.S. Army personnel joined in the tent search. The pilots and mechanics, meanwhile, using the superior weapons supplied by the Marines, also targeted the Japanese with a vengeance.

Hudson and Crim continued attacking together, firing and killing every enemy soldier in sight. Moving in tandem towards a ravine on the other side of the camp, the duo spotted a pillbox in a nearby trench. While the Army checked the airmen's tents, Hudson and Crim decided to check the pillbox. Any Japanese inside were about to get shot.

As they crouched down and approached, a Japanese soldier reached out of the pillbox and tossed a grenade at Hudson. Hudson tried to maneuver out of the way, but the grenade exploded at point-blank range, blowing off his helmet, three of his fingers, and destroying his carbine. He was alive, but had been taken out of the fight.

Crim had to think fast. His comrade needed help, and he needed it now. As the Army and Marines turned up the heat on the Japanese, Crim locked arms under his commanding officer and started dragging Hudson across the camp toward the field hospital.

Meanwhile, a Marine tank rolled into the area, first positioning at the top of the hill and then moving into the trench, taking aim at the pillbox, which would be the enemy's last line of defense. By now, more troops from the U.S. Army's 147th Infantry were joining the fight that had spread throughout the camp. Overwhelmed by the Americans' surging numbers, it was only a matter of time before the Japanese were defeated. The fire from the Marines' tank, combined with the rifle fire from Army and Marine units, broke the back of the enemy. With a handful of exceptions, any Japanese not killed in the firefight committed suicide.

By nine a.m., the bodies of ninety-eight Japanese lay strewn throughout the Twenty-First Group's compound. Another 232 dead Japanese were scattered across the ravines, bomb craters and on the open ground. More lay around the pillbox which the Marines and Army had blistered with bullets and grenades. Eighteen Japanese had been captured—the last of their army left alive on the island.

With the surprise massacre finally extinguished, the Americans' victory on Iwo Jima was complete. But the price had been devastating. Forty-four members of the command had been killed, including eleven pilots. Upwards of a hundred airmen were wounded. Some eventually returned from the hospital to fly again. Dr. Hart, the only medical officer on duty near Central Field, later received a Silver Star for his heroics. Crim, meanwhile, replaced the wounded Hudson as commanding officer of the 531st Fighter Squadron; he would lead the Twenty-First Group on its first mission the next day: the strafing of Haha Jima.

CHAPTER 11

Jerry Hopes for a Chance

March 30, 1945

On March 30, 1945, General Moore ordered a large group of Mustangs to execute a round-trip practice fight from Iwo Jima to Saipan. Knowing the first strike on Japan was just days away, Moore wanted to test his Mustangs to see how they'd hold up under longer flight conditions. The one-way flight from Saipan to Iwo Jima was 725 miles, only twenty-five miles shorter than the distance from Iwo Jima to Japan. It was actually the same route Jerry, Beckwith, and others had taken when they first arrived on Iwo Jima from Saipan. Then, distance hadn't been an issue, since they planned on landing at Iwo Jima rather than turning around and flying back to Saipan. On the planned trips to Japan, of course, there would be no opportunity to land halfway—not if the pilots wanted to come back alive, anyway. The round-trip mission to Japan would take eight hours and be arduous on both Moore's pilots and their planes. The P-51s had never been pushed to such limits. Hence, Moore and General LeMay wanted to get at least one "practice run" under the pilots' belts.

Moore selected a hundred pilots for the test flight, including Jerry. Although being picked for the test flight did not mean automatic selection for the actual mission to Japan, those chosen held out hope that if they performed well on the test flight, they would be included.

That, however, turned out to be a big "if."

The results of the test flight were disappointing. Mechanical problems forced a number of P-51s to land in Saipan, unable to complete the round-trip journey. Others had to turn and fly back to Iwo Jima before even reaching Saipan. Altogether, nearly half of the P-51s on the test flight failed to complete the round-trip.

The development raised concerns for LeMay and Moore. They'd known from the beginning that with such a large amount of planes in the sky, it would be hard to achieve across-the-board perfection on a test run. But issues—even minor ones—with fifty percent of the planes proved worse than they'd anticipated. And if one factored in Japanese fighters and ground-based antiaircraft that would be launching enemy fire toward the American planes, the potential problems compounded. Soon, all the planes that started the test flight were back on Iwo Jima, and Moore put his squadron mechanics and planners to work on identifying problems that had occurred during the test flight, with instructions to engage in aggressive problem-solving and corrective procedures.

Jerry, meanwhile, had been one of those who managed to complete the test flight to Saipan and back without encountering any problems. He hoped this would catch his commanding officer's attention and guarantee him a slot in the big mission.

But he was dealing in a world with no guarantees.

As March gave way to April, the anticipation among the American pilots stationed on Iwo Jima reached its highest point since their arrival. The date had been set for their first, massive, joint air raid on Japan with the B-29s: April 7.

At long last, this was it.

But when April arrived, it brought something else: rain. The first four days of the month, it rained so heavily and frequently that no flight operations were conducted. After a month of near-perfect weather, it now seemed like the rain would never stop.

And so the men of the Seventh Fighter Command, anxious and ready to fly, were subjected to yet another form of discomfort. Based on weather forecasts, the mission date had been circled on the calendar. Their hearts pounded each time they looked at it, hoping to see their names on the mission list. Three hundred were competing for a mission of only one hundred slots.

For the next few days, Jerry could only bide his time and focus as the intelligence officers revealed plans for the attack. The pilots gathered under the primitive Quonset hut that had been erected for intelligence briefings and received information about the specific target for the mission: the Nakajima Aircraft Engine Factories west of Tokyo. Those factories had built engines for at least thirty-seven different military aircraft, mostly fighter and bombers, including Kamikaze aircraft that had been flown into U.S. ships. Taking the plants out would be a significant step in crippling the Japanese war machine.

The announcement of the target selection heightened the pilots' excitement. Though they were still unsure who would fly the mission, each man had to be ready.

Always be ready. Always do your best. These were the words Jerry already lived by.

If only he could get selected.

CHAPTER 12

The Rain—and News—Breaks

Seventy-Eighth Fighter Squadron Headquarters
Iwo Jima
April 6, 1945

"**O**kay, gentlemen. Gather round."

Major Jim Vande Hey, the twenty-nine-year-old commanding officer of the Seventy-Eighth Fighter Squadron, was a man's man and a pilot's pilot. The young man bore a special, no-nonsense charisma that commanded respect, and, when he spoke, attention. For Vande Hey, the war against Japan had been personal from its inception. On the morning of December 7, 1941, as a twenty-three-year-old second lieutenant and recent graduate of pilot training, he'd sat on his bunk at Wheeler Army Airfield, the main U.S. Army Air Force fighter base in Hawaii, talking with a buddy before heading to church. As the sound of aircraft began buzzing overhead outside his barracks, Vande Hey and his comrades thought they were U.S. Navy pilots, who frequently flew over the U.S. Army's aviation barracks on the weekends in a good-natured effort to stoke the intra-service rivalry. The Army guys usually returned the favor, buzzing over the

Navy barracks at Ford Field or Kanaoe Naval Air station when it was their turn to fly later in the afternoon.

This time, however, the sound was quickly accompanied by the shrill, whistling sounds of falling bombs. A second later, thunderous explosions rocked the earth. Vande Hey and his buddies knew then the planes overhead were not piloted by Americans. Wheeler Army Airfield was the first target of Japanese dive bombers on that fateful morning of December 7, 1941. The Japanese struck the airfield before moving on to the Navy ships at Pearl Harbor, hoping to prevent the American warplanes at Wheeler from engaging them. The results of the surprise attack on Wheeler devastated the base's air capabilities: of 146 operational aircraft on the field before the attack, seventy-six were totally destroyed.

The Japanese continued to bomb the airfield throughout their assault on Pearl Harbor, making it almost impossible to get aircraft off the ground. And yet, somehow, twelve pilots assigned to the Fifteenth Pursuit Group at Wheeler succeeded in getting their P-36 Hawks and P-40 Warhawks in the air. These pilots engaged the Japanese in furious dogfights and scored some of the first American victories of World War II. But tragedy still marked the day: thirty-three airmen were killed at Wheeler Field, and many others were injured. Vande Hey was fortunate; he survived the Japanese bombs and bullets. But he would not forget impressions of the death, carnage and destruction caused by the enemy.

Nor would he forget what happened after the Japanese left Wheeler Field and Pearl Harbor a burning heap. Just ten hours later, news arrived that the Japanese had begun their invasion of the Philippines, which made the Japanese aggression even more personal to the young pilot. Vande Hey had spent time attending college there and had numerous friends in the country, many of whom, through no fault of their own, were now subjects of bloodthirsty Japanese thuggery.

Today, on Iwo Jima, Vande Hey looked his men in the eyes and delivered the news: they would fly to Japan in the morning as scheduled. His audience cheered, and he continued. The Americans would take sixteen planes per squadron as part of the attack force. That meant ninety-eight pilots would sweep north, under strict radio silence, guarding the bombers. Ten more Mustangs would fly in reserve, circling over the ocean just off the coast and ready to go in over Japan if a plane in the main fleet could not complete the task. The commanding officers looked primarily at pilot experience to determine who would fly first. Those selected would need to be ready to depart at seven a.m.

Vande Hey started to read the names of those men, who, whether they lived or died, were about to become part of history.

"Tapp."

"Roseberry."

"Yellin."

At the sound of his name, Jerry felt a surge of energy. He was going to war against the heart of Japan.

He listened carefully to the preflight briefing from the intelligence officer: once reaching the Japanese coastline with the B-29s, the Mustangs would climb to thirty thousand feet. Their job would be to watch the bombers topside. If a Japanese plane tried to climb high and take out one of the B-29s from above, the Japanese pilots would have to deal with the American guard first.

It would be the mission of a lifetime.

Now, if only he could manage a good night's sleep.

CHAPTER 13

On to Japan

Saturday, April 7, 1945

When the crest of the orange sun broke over the Pacific at 5:22 a.m. on April 7, Jerry was up, wired, and ready to get into the air. In a war zone, the dawn always brought a measure of uncertainty. There could be bigger days to follow, or this could be his last day on earth. Even at twenty-one, Jerry had learned that no man could totally control his destiny. A million things could go wrong today: mechanical failure, bad weather, antiaircraft fire, a sudden influx of enemy forces with no escape route for the *Dorrie R* and her companions. Jerry had already seen more than enough death to know that not a single day should be taken for granted.

But this knowledge didn't make him afraid to live, or to do what he came to do.

The three hundred B-29 bombers that Jerry and his fighter group were going to protect today were already in the air, having taken off in the dark hours of the morning from Saipan. Jerry headed over to the Quonset hut for the final briefing: while the main force of B-29s would bomb the aircraft factories, another handful of B-29s and P-61s would fly alongside the P-51s to Japan, solely for the purpose of providing navigation for the P-51s (both the P-61s and the B-29s had radar/tracking systems). That smaller group of B-29s would not fly over Japan; rather, they would remain offshore while the invasion force carried out its strikes, then help navigate the fighters back to Iwo Jima once the bombing mission was complete. Also, in addition to the backup Mustangs, eight more P-51s would provide "top cover" for the rescue U.S. submarine below, as well as the B-29 navigators at the rally point just off Japan. The backup planes not called on for the attack over Japan would then turn back to Iwo Jima, accompanied by the P-61s.

Before long, Jerry was strapped into the cockpit of the *Dorrie R* as it sat on the airfield. He glanced out at the other Mustangs, all awaiting the *go* signal. The B-29s were approaching, the pilots knew, somewhere in the southern skies. And soon they appeared, an incredible sight of over a hundred single-engine fighter planes, painted in their aviation battle gray.

Jerry looked down at his grounds crewmen. Thumbs up were exchanged, and then at seven a.m. precisely came the signal for the planes to start their engines. Jerry fired up the *Dorrie R,* and the hum of her seventeen-hundred-horsepower engine joined the roaring chorus filling the air. The sound grew into a thunder so great that it shook the ground. The ground controllers began to motion the pilots into a takeoff position. One by one, the P-51s began rushing down the runway and lifting into the morning sky.

Picking up more speed and slicing through a slight layer of ground fog, the wheels of the *Dorrie R* broke contact with the earth. The end of Airfield No. 1 disappeared under her wings, and the Mustang nosed upward. A moment later, Jerry pulled her out of the takeoff line and over the ocean, the distinctive granite features of Mount Suribachi now down to his right. He swung the *Dorrie R* around and lined up in the "four finger" formation, assuming the "wingman" position with the Yellow Flight. The first leg of the flight plan called for a rendezvous with the B-29s over Kita Iwo Jima, or "North Sulfur Island"—the small, jagged area of about two square miles located approximately fifty miles north of Iwo Jima. Once this had been accomplished, the fleet turned toward Tokyo.

Because of the long range of the mission, the Mustangs were carrying two supplemental 110-gallon fuel tanks, one under each wing, enough fuel for the initial flight to Japan. As the Japanese coastline came into sight, each P-51 hit a switch that dropped the spent fuel tanks into the bay. The tanks had served their purpose; now, the planes needed to lighten their load for the upcoming dogfight with enemy aircraft.

The planes began crossing Suruga Bay, one of the two great inland bays in the Americans' flight path. To the west of the bay was the Japanese mainland. Off to the north, Jerry witnessed, for the first time, a landmark he'd seen so often in pictures: the great, snow-capped peak of Mount Fuji, looming twelve thousand feet into the sky. He remembered the intelligence officer's briefing from the previous morning: "When you fly across Suruga Bay, focus your gun cameras on the tip of Mount Fuji. In that way, we will be able to evaluate your film when you fire your guns at the enemy."

Jerry trained his .50-caliber guns on the mountain, and felt a sense of excitement, knowing that the city of Tokyo awaited just seventy miles beyond. On a clear day, they said, that great snow-capped mountain could easily be seen from the Japanese capital city. The Americans' flight path would take them near some of Japan's most populated areas: the neck of the Izu Peninsula (between Suruga Bay and Sagami Bay), past the Yokosuka peninsula (between Sagami Bay and Tokyo Bay), and then, once they crossed the Tokyo Bay, the land surrounding Tokyo, and the city itself. The projected time over the target, if all went well, was estimated to be about fifteen minutes. However, no one expected the Japanese to wait until the planes were over their target before striking.

By design, the Seventy-Eighth Fighter Squadron flew in the right front quarter of the Americans' formation as they soared closer to

Tokyo. The prime position was largely due to Vande Hey's and Jim Tapp's reputations as pilots; General Moore knew that they would make a formidable "one-two" punch, and based on military intelligence, the general believed that the Japanese had no pilots who could match them. The spot in the formation meant the Seventy-Eighth would be the first to fly over Japan; it also meant they might catch the first waves of Japanese Zeros awaiting the American aircraft. The American command, frankly, hoped that the Japanese planes *would* come out and fight. An experienced Mustang pilot would trump an experienced Zero pilot. Nearly four years after Pearl Harbor, the Americans had the superior fighter planes. Nothing in the world could trump the P-51 Mustang. If the Zeroes came out en masse, perhaps the P-51s could inflict significant damage to the Japanese air defenses in one mission.

At 10:20 a.m., as the Americans flew over the waters of Suruga Bay, the first enemy fighter appeared. The Ki-44 Shōki, referred to as a "Tojo" Fighter, approached quickly from the west, flying in on a hostile vector from the Japanese mainland. Its target was the American B-29s. The heavily armed Tojo carried four 12.7-millimeter machine guns (some Tojos also had two twenty-millimeter cannons). If it got a clear shot at a B-29, its guns were lethal. In addition, plane's agility made it a dangerous threat to American bombers.

The question mark when facing these war machines, however, was the competency of the Japanese pilots. Since 1942, the Japanese airmen had taken a pounding when going up against the air defense of the U.S. Marines and the pilots of the U.S. Navy. Beginning with the battle of Midway, when the outnumbered U.S. Navy struck a severe blow against the Japanese by sinking all four aircraft carriers in the Japanese task force, Japan suffered a loss from which she would never recover. U.S. military intelligence believed that many of Japan's better and more experienced pilots had been killed earlier in the war and that the P-51s today would be facing less experienced pilots compared, for example, to those who had attacked Pearl Harbor.

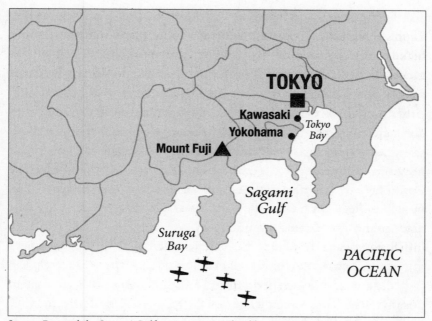

Suruga Bay and the Sagami Gulf are two great inland bays near the landmark Mount Fuji.

Now the Blue Flight of the Forty-Sixth Fighter Squadron broke off and gave chase to the Tojo, becoming the first American squadron to open fire on the Japanese over Japan. The American quartet scored multiple hits against the outnumbered enemy aircraft, and watched as the Japanese fighter veered away.

Within minutes, however, a Japanese Ki-45 Toryu "Dragon Slayer" managed to penetrate too close into the Americans' air space. The tip of the American air armada had flown within five minutes of Tokyo when something told Major John Piper, the commanding officer of the Forty-Seventh squadron, to look overhead. Piper spotted the Dragon Slayer about a thousand feet above the American planes, ready to strike. The aircraft—a twin-engine, heavily armed, long-range fighter—was one of Japan's best weapons against the B-29.

The Americans had to get the Dragon Slayer out of there.

Piper pulled up on his stick, and the other three planes in his Red Flight broke into a pursuit maneuver. The Dragon Slayer, outnumbered four to one, would have nothing of it. As soon as the Mustangs locked in, the Dragon Slayer initiated a steep dive, rushing toward the waters of the bay. Piper and his men had to make a quick decision: either they chase the Ki-45 all the way down to the water, and probably catch and destroy him, or they remain on post at eighteen thousand feet to continue protecting the B-29s. With the Dragon Slayer now out of play, Piper's squadron chose to resume their defensive position guarding the B-29s. As much as Piper wanted to give chase, he had to keep his eye on the ball. He and his men were there, first and foremost, to protect bombers.

The pattern repeated as the Americans crossed Suruga Bay: more interceptors appeared, only to be taken down by the P-51s.

Meanwhile, the men of the Seventy-Eighth, despite their prominent position, had yet to be challenged by the Japanese. By 10:30 a.m., they had crossed over from Suruga Bay to Sagami Bay. As the planes made landfall for the final phase before the attack, Japanese antiaircraft fire picked up considerably. Down below and out front, the sky began to fill with waves of black streaks and smoke rising from the ground.

Over in Yellow Flight, Jerry kept his hands on his yoke and eyes peeled on the horizon for incoming enemy craft.

Below, the industrial area of the Nakajima Aircraft Engine Factory came into view. The sight from the late morning sky resembled the photographs the pilots had studied in their intelligence briefings. From the air, the buildings of Japan spread over several acres, a labyrinth of squares and rectangles rising from the ground. Within minutes, the men of the Seventy-Eighth had led the bombers over their targets, and now, from their position high above, they held the best vantage point in the world for watching the bombers do their work.

"I saw little dots of light spring from the ground as the bombs exploded," Jerry wrote later.[1] "Wave after wave of bombers dropped their cargo inside the squares of fire on the ground. We fighter pilots were in a constant state of alert; Japanese fighters were all over the sky and the aerial battles between us were fierce. We had to protect our 'Big Brothers'—the B-29s as they droned on and on over the target. When I had a chance to look down, I could see fires raging. All of the city, it seemed, was on fire."

Just as the B-29s opened fire, Tapp spotted yet another Dragon Slayer nearby, vectoring into attack mode—the Seventy-Eighth's first opportunity for engagement. Tapp broke off in pursuit. Maneuvering his Mustang into close range, Tapp opened fire, his bullets ripping into the enemy aircraft's engine. Tapp's wingman, Lieutenant Maher, also opened fire, but it wasn't clear if he scored a hit. Tapp, meanwhile, knew his fire had struck the plane, but didn't know if he'd destroyed it. Having chased the Dragon Slayer out of the way, he and Maher pulled back up to twenty thousand feet to resume their protective position of the bombers.

A second threat swooped in, however, this time a Kawasaki single-engine Ki-61 Hein, identified by the U.S. Air Force as a "Tony." Externally, the Tony presented a long, sleek-looking design, with the cockpit set well behind the engine in the center-forward position. Faster and more maneuverable than the twin-engine Dragon Slayer, the Tony—which looked almost like the P-51s—could strike with quick and lethal effectiveness. Tapp had to take it out or risk losing a slew of bombers.

The pilot pushed down on his plane's throttle to close the gap between the two aircraft, then pulled back to avoid overflying the target. After closing within a thousand feet of the Tony, Tapp opened fire. The enemy craft burst into flames, and Tapp pulled away. It was his first sure shoot-down—known as a "kill" in military aviation—of the day. The pilot turned around a second later and saw the Japanese pilot bail out, his parachute deploying and his body dangling down below.

There was no rest, however, for the American pilot. Tapp noticed a B-29 under fire by an unidentified enemy fighter attacking the bomber from the rear. He tightened his circle, and getting an angle on the Japanese fighter, opened fire. The enemy aircraft burst into flames, began spinning out of control, and fell to earth.

Kill number two.

The Japanese planes were everywhere, it seemed. Six more (this time, single-engine fighters) approached. Tapp bore down on one of them and opened fire again. A second later, the Japanese plane broke up, its wing splintering off, both the plane and wing soon crashing below. It marked the third plane Tapp had downed within minutes. He also actually fired at a fourth plane and struck it but hadn't realized it had been shot down. He was later given credit for the kill after other pilots reported it. Overall, his heroism that day would go down as one of the greatest feats in the history of the Air Force.

The B-29s lingered for a total of forty-five minutes over Tokyo, unloading their fire on the Nakajima Aircraft Engine Factory and other targets and reducing them to seas of burning rubble. As always, however, there was a cost: "The fighting and the flak was intense," Jerry described later.[2] "At one point I saw one of our B-29s get hit, and the right wing fell off. The plane burst into flames, and then, as if it was all being photographed in slow motion, one parachute came out, then a second, and a third; then the huge, lumbering plane just keeled over like a ship in the water, went into a spin, and fell from the sky. Of the twelve crew members on board, only three had bailed out."

As their bombing on Tokyo concluded, the B-29s and their P-51 escorts began turning south for the flight back to Iwo Jima. Halfway between Tokyo and Mount Fuji, a call came in over the radio from one of the B-29s.

"Bushmaster Leader! We got an inbound bogey approaching from 12 o'clock high! Repeat, inbound bogey at 12 o'clock high!"

The phrase "12 o'clock high" was used among American military aviation personnel to describe the location of attacking enemy aircraft based on the imagery of a clock face. The bomber was considered the center; the term "high" meant above the bomber, while "level" meant at the same altitude and "low" meant the enemy was below the bomber. Enemy fighter pilots preferred this "12 o'clock high" location, because the target aircraft had difficulty spotting the attacking fighter, which was in the bomber's "blind spot." For the aggressor, this proved the best position from which to get a shot at the bomber's wings and engines.

Vande Hey looked up through the top of the Mustang's glass cockpit into the blue skies above. Sure enough, the twin-engine Japanese Ki-45 "Dragon Slayer" was about to take a shot at the B-29.

Vande Hey pulled back on the stick of his plane, *Jeanne VII,* and put it in a climb, bringing the Dragon Slayer into his gun sights. He fired a quick burst from his .50-caliber, striking the aircraft and sending it into an evasive maneuver. Not a shoot-down, but good enough for the time being. The threat, at least, had been removed.

A minute later, he spotted a twin-engine Japanese Ki-46 "Dinah" moving in. It made a diving turn to the right, again, targeting the American bombers.

Vande Hey set an immediate intercept course, closed on the enemy, and opened fire. This time, his bullets sprayed into the engine and right wing of the enemy aircraft. Debris flew off the plane, and the Dinah burst into flames. Vande Hey quickly broke off to avoid a mid-air collision with the crippled fighter. Jerry, soaring several hundred feet above with the Yellow Flight, saw the Dinah fall to the earth. The shoot-down of the Dinah marked Vande Hey's third confirmed kill of the war.

The pilot rejoined his squadron, which pushed on toward Iwo Jima. Remarkably, the American P-51 pilots' casualties for their first mission over Japan had been low. One pilot did not return: the P-51 flown by Lieutenant Robert Anderson from the 531st Squadron was spotted by his fellow pilots burning and on a crash pattern over

Tokyo. Anderson never bailed out and lost his life that day. A second P-51, flown by Captain Frank Ayers of the Forty-Seventh Squadron pilot, ran out of fuel on the flight back to Iwo Jima. Captain Ayers was more fortunate than Anderson—he bailed out near the U.S. Navy destroyer on watch in waters just north of Iwo Jima and was picked up by a U.S. Navy search-and-rescue team. Meanwhile, Jerry and the rest of the Seventy-Eighth landed back at Iwo Jima without losing a single plane from their squadron.

Later that evening, after hitting the hot tubs and grabbing a hot meal, Jerry and his squadron mates attended the post-mission intelligence de-briefing in the squadron Quonset hut. There, they learned that only three B-29s—out of the hundred that had flown the mission—had been lost. By contrast, at least twenty-one Japanese fighter aircraft had been shot out of the skies over the Japanese mainland, and the B-29s had unloaded tons of deadly and destructive fire on Japanese ground targets.

All in all, the first joint long-range mission against the Japanese homeland had been a smashing success, with the American pilots inflicting far more damage on the enemy than they had suffered. Eventually, the air raid of April 7 would be remembered as the greatest accomplishment in the history of the Seventh Fighter Command. Just as their fellow patriots had done at Normandy, these pilots had taken the fight directly to the shores of the enemy under heavy fire. Many of the men also enjoyed a bit of personal satisfaction that the raid had come on April 7, subtle vengeance for what the Japanese had inflicted on December 7, 1941, at Pearl Harbor.

But the stubborn Japanese were far from finished. Brainwashed into a kamikaze mentality and prepared to commit suicide for their emperor, they refused to surrender, and remained capable of dealing a deadly blow to the Americans.

This would be a long air-war of attrition, the American intelligence officers told their pilots that night, followed by a dreaded invasion of the Japanese homeland itself. For Jerry and the men of the Seventy-Eighth, the real war was just beginning. Mortal danger, as always, loomed over the horizon.

CHAPTER 14

The Second Empire Mission and the Death of a President

April 12, 1945

A long with the destruction of key Japanese targets, the April 7 mission had accomplished another tactical purpose: it proved that the long, round-trip mission could be made and effective. The rest of April and May brought more fighter-accompanied bombing runs against Japan, shaking the island to its core and laying the groundwork for a U.S. invasion. Every day, it seemed, Jerry piloted the *Dorrie R* through the Pacific skies, alternating between attacks on Chichi Jima and Japan.

Meanwhile, news arrived from the States and from Europe, reminding the men living inside this temporary hell how much the world was changing on distant shores. Perhaps the largest collective shock came just five days after their first great mission. On April 12, 1945, a radio announcement from CBS interrupted regular programming of "The American Frontier with the Western Family and Daniel Boone":

We interrupt this program to bring you a special news bulletin from CBS World News. A press association has just announced that President Roosevelt is dead. The President died of a cerebral hemorrhage. All we know so far is that the President died in Warm Springs, in Georgia.

The message spread like wildfire across the globe. On Iwo Jima, the Americans were stunned. A profound mourning followed. FDR had been a highly controversial president, but to many of these pilots—who had known no other presidents and knew little of politics except their country had been attacked—Roosevelt had, in a way, been a comforting father-figure. He was also their commander-in-chief.

Increasing their anguish that day on the island were several losses within their own ranks. April 12 marked the Seventh Fighter Group's second long-range mission to Japan. With windy conditions at takeoff, this second mission did not begin as smoothly as the first nor progress nearly as well. Several pilots, including Second Lieutenant Maurice F. Gourley of the Forty-Seventh Fighter Squadron and First Lieutenant Gordon A. Christoe of Jerry's Seventy-Eighth, were shot down and killed over Tokyo. First Lieutenant Fred White, flying as Tapp's wingman, was another casualty. Tapp had been leading his flight group off the far right of the B-29 fleet over Tokyo when he looked down and spotted a Japanese "Tony" moving into firing position. Tapp accelerated downward and got the Tony into his gun sights. White, as Tapp's loyal wingman, executed a crisp maneuver to follow his boss down toward the target. Tapp wasted no time opening fire on the enemy fighter, and the Tony fell from the sky. Unfortunately, however, White's shadow maneuver behind Tapp was a bit too close—spent cartridges from Tapp's wing-mounted .50-caliber machine gun got sucked into White's engine, creating an instant mechanical problem.

Tapp recognized the problem immediately and knew he had to get his wingman away from Japan. Bailing over the ocean was much preferable to doing so over Tokyo and becoming a POW.

With White still on his wing, Tapp swung his Mustang around in a wide circle and set his back out towards the Pacific. Within minutes, the two aircraft had cleared the Japanese shoreline. White's Mustang may not make it far, but there were also designated rescue points in the ocean, with a U.S. Navy warship and two American submarines pre-positioned for rescue purposes.

White's plane began to leak coolant as it struggled against headwinds. From the glass canopy of his P-51, Tapp saw more and more fluid spraying from White's engine, creating a long line in the sky behind the plane. Tapp recognized the plane would never make it back to Iwo Jima. Both pilots, however, knew the drill for engine failure over water. Unlike larger aircraft such as long-range bombers or cargo planes, where ditching the plane into the sea might be viable, fighter planes would not float for any length of time, and the P-51, with its air-scoop under its fuselage, would sink faster than most fighters. In fact, according to the P-51's operations manual, the plane might, in a lucky scenario, stay on the surface for one and a half to two seconds before sinking. In this instance, a P-51 pilot's best option was to bail. Inside the cockpit of the dying Mustang, White recognized the move as his only chance for survival.

Tapp vectored a course over the position of one of the rescue submarines and signaled for White to bail out. Hopefully the American submarine, still submerged somewhere under the Philippine Sea, would surface and pick him up.

The leader and his wingman exchanged thumbs up. White pulled the emergency release handle, located on the right forward side of the cockpit, all the way back to release the canopy.

Tapp watched as the glass bubble covering the cockpit flew off White's plane. A moment later, White climbed out of the plane and jumped.

He was free-falling in the sky, thousands of feet above the water.

Tapp kept his eyes on his friend, waiting for his parachute to open. He waited. And waited.

White kept falling, dropping like a rock. He plunged toward the ocean.

Come on. Open up, baby! Open!

But his parachute never deployed. When White smashed into the water, he died almost instantaneously on contact. His body would never be recovered.

■ ■ ■

Jerry took White's death hard.

They were a tight-knit bunch, the men of the Seventy-Eighth—a group who helped one another and watched one another's backs. Just as Tapp had helped mentor Jerry, so, too, had Jerry helped guide some of the younger pilots, including White. Back in Hawaii, he'd trained White in combat flight procedures as a wingman for D-Flight, another moniker for the fourth group of planes in the sixteen-plane formation. The training involved many hours practicing in the air, with their planes flying side-by-side over Hawaii and the Pacific. During the flights, Jerry taught him to hug the element leader's wing, and White rehearsed intricate crisscrossing maneuvers designed for the wingman to evade enemy fire. Thus, in many respects, it had been Jerry who trained White for combat.

Through all of this, they had become like family, just like the rest of the Seventy-Eighth. They lived together, fought together, trained together. When one of them died, a part of all of them died. And when White plummeted into the Pacific, a part of Jerry went down with him.

But there had been three pilots total from the squadron lost that day, and each one stung their remaining comrades, reminding the survivors of their own mortality. Freedom exacted a heavy price: the loss of friends, physical discomfort, emotional anguish—even the time to properly grieve. A war zone did not allow for much mourning. For the men on Iwo Jima, the fight would march on, and so would they, determined to finish what they had started.

For Major James M. Vande Hey, the mission would mark his last as commander of the Seventy-Eighth Figher Squadron, as orders to a new duty station were imminent for him.

CHAPTER 15

Baseball, Softball, and the Southern Boy from Clemson

May 29, 1945

For Jerry, reaching out to mentor younger pilots seemed a natural thing. He felt a duty to pass on the knowledge he'd acquired and a passion for equipping these younger pilots with the aerial combat skills necessary to survive the war. Jerry had seen far too much tragedy already. If he could teach them an extra trick or two, it might be the difference between life and death.

But perhaps he also wanted to make sure that none of the newer pilots felt ostracized in the way he had in his hometown on the memorable morning way back in 1936. Already, he'd started mentoring fellow Seventy-Eighth squadron pilot Phil Schlamberg, in part because of their common Jewish heritage, but also because Phil seemed like a loner. Both traits made Jerry feel protective of Phil. But Jerry also bonded with others, like First Lieutenant Danny Mathis Jr. Danny had attended secondary school in Augusta, Georgia, before enrolling at Clemson University in South Carolina in 1940. A skinny, brown-headed kid with a sharp chin, he'd graduated in 1944—shortly before D-Day—with a degree in agriculture. Like so many of the young pilots in the Seventy-Eighth, because Danny showed promise as an aviator, the Army (in which he'd enrolled) accelerated him through flight school.

When Danny first showed up as a rookie pilot with the Seventy-Eighth in Hawaii, one of the first things Jerry noticed about him— aside from his thick, Southern drawl—was that Danny played a mean game of baseball, or, in this case, softball. Jerry had been an accomplished second baseman in school, and the soft-talking Mathis was a lightning-quick shortstop who also swung a good bat. They proved a devastating infield combination for the Seventy-Eighth Fighter Squadron softball team in Hawaii. But they also became good friends. Danny often flew as Jerry's wingman, and on May 29, as the Seventy-Eighth prepared for a bombing attack against Yokohama—the great Japanese port city on Tokyo Bay—he was slated to do so again.

As the home of the Imperial Japanese Naval Academy and head-quarters for the Imperial Japanese fleet, Yokohama was of high strategic importance to Japan. The Yokosuka Naval Arsenal, one of the major naval shipyards, was also located nearby, just south of the port city. With a fleet of over four hundred B-29 bombers, the American command intended to blister the Japanese industry at Yokohama and set the city ablaze. The bombers would be accompanied by men in the Fifteenth and Twenty-First Fighter Groups, including Jerry and Danny.

That morning of May 29, the Empire of Japan already found itself in a precarious spot. Twenty-one days had passed since its Axis ally, Nazi Germany, had fallen to the Allies. With Germany finished, America would now pull forces from Europe and pour its full fury on Japan. Previously, the Japanese had felt the mettle of the U.S. Navy and Marine Corps, and on this very day, Marines were plowing across the island of Okinawa, soon to capture Shuri Castle.

Meanwhile, back in April, the American air forces on Iwo Jima had inflicted significant damage on another key military target:

Atsugi Naval Airfield, located on the east coast of Japan and twenty-five miles southwest of Tokyo. Three years before Pearl Harbor, the Japanese Navy had began construction of a large air base that would house the Japanese 302 Naval Aviation Corps, which became one of Japan's most formidable and destructive fighter squadrons during World War II. Atsugi-based aircraft shot down more than three hundred American bombers during the fire bombings of 1945. The Americans' April mission against Atsugi—its third great Empire Mission—had dealt the Japanese another blow: their strike destroyed twenty-three enemy planes in the air, another fourteen on the ground, and damaged fifty more.

Today, unbeknownst to the Japanese, the U.S. Army Air Force was about to pay them another visit.

At 6:30 a.m., the *Dorrie R* nosed off Airfield No. 1 for what felt like its thousandth mission to Jerry, who'd now been on Iwo Jima for two-and-a-half months. He wondered, often, if this war would ever end. He checked out the side of his cockpit and saw that he'd been joined in the air by Mathis. They exchanged the traditional thumbs up and set their course to join the rest of the planes for the approximately seven-hundred-mile trek.

Midway through the flight to Japan, the squadrons ran into bad weather. When flying head-on towards a storm front, a pilot had three options: try flying around it, over it, or under it. All, of course, carried risk. The system might be too big to fly around, and a P-51, especially on a long-range mission where fuel would be stretched even in a straight shot, could run out of gas prematurely. Flying over the cell, however, wasn't optimal, because the top of the system might be above the effective ceiling of the aircraft. Depending on how low the cloud cover came to the sea, going below the storm posed its own problems: a pilot ran the risk of down-drafts and strong winds if he tried that route. But there was also a saying in aviation for such situations: "When you're damned if you do and damned if you don't, pick a damn."

In this case, the group decided to attempt flying under the weather front.

Following the lead of their B-29 navigation plane, Jerry, Danny, and the other squadron members pushed down on their yokes, executing a dive designed to bring them just two thousand feet above the water. Though the route was bumpy, they cleared the bottom of the cloud cover with enough open air space to continue on to Japan.

Some three and a half hours after departing Iwo Jima, the Mustangs arrived off the Japanese coast, ahead of the B-29s flying in from the Marianas and designated to provide the firepower on the mission. Waiting for the bombers to arrive, the Mustangs fell into a holding pattern off the Japanese shoreline. A nervous anticipation soon blanketed the fighter groups. Everybody was worried about fuel. Jerry checked his gauge. Hopefully, the bombers would show soon. Nobody wanted to ditch a Mustang into the ocean, and, after what happened with White's parachute, nobody wanted to bail out of one either.

A moment later, a gorgeous sight broke into the skies from the south: the lead elements of the B-29s emerged from the cloud cover. The P-51s soon took their positions, and, together, the planes set a course due east that would take them over Mount Fuji towards Yokohama.

Within minutes, Japanese interceptors could be seen, coming out to challenge them. Reaching their target, the B-29s began to drop their payload as the Mustangs started engaging the Japanese fighters over the city and Tokyo Bay. Smoke and fire rose as the P-51s made waste of their Japanese opposition. In early combat operations, the Japanese "Zero" had established a legendary reputation as a dogfighter, with initial kill ratios of twelve to one. But by mid-1942, a combination of new tactics and the introduction of better equipment enabled the Allied pilots to engage the Zero on more equal terms. In fact, the P-51 was a superior craft. But an aerial dogfight also required piloting and marksmanship skills, factors that came into play as much as the quality of the aircraft. Not a single member of the Seventy-Eighth would take the sight of a Zero lightly.

Patrolling out on the right flank of the B-29s, both Jerry and Danny kept their eyes peeled for movement in their zone.

It happened in an instant. A Zero penetrated the sector, threatening every aircraft in Jerry's zone. Jerry jerked the control stick and brought the *Dorrie R* into pursuit mode. Danny followed. Jerry opened fire on the enemy craft, then Danny. A long stream of smoke billowed from the Japanese plane as it spun out of control, dropping down to the city below. The infield duo had just scored their first aerial victory of the war.

The campaign, in fact, was ultimately successful for the entire fleet. That evening, after they returned to Iwo Jima, Jerry learned during the intelligence de-briefing that in just one hour and nine minutes, firebombs from over 450 U.S. bombers had reduced forty-two percent of the Japanese city to rubble. His friend and former squadron-mate, Captain Todd "Baby Face" Moore, had single-handedly shot down three Japanese interceptors, tallying the highest kill-count for the mission and placing him neck-and-neck with Tapp for the most number of kills over Tokyo. Altogether, the Mustangs had shot down at least twenty-six enemy aircraft, possibly as many as thirty-five. Another twenty-three had been damaged in the air. The downside: of the 101 Mustangs, three had been lost, and two pilots were missing. Despite the horror of their unknown fate, Yokohama had been the unit's most devastating coordinated assault yet on Japan.

In just two more days, on June 1, they would try it again. The Seventh Fighter Command planned its largest all-out attack to date, unleashing not only the Fifteenth and Twenty-First Fighter Groups, but also for the first time, the newly-deployed 506th.

That day, however, would turn out far differently than Jerry—even trained to expect the unexpected—could anticipate.

CHAPTER 16

The Raid on Osaka

June 1, 1945

"You're grounded for this mission."

Those weren't the words Jerry expected, nor hoped to hear. However, Doc Lipshitz, the group's dental officer, was putting his foot down. Jerry's four wisdom teeth had been tormenting him for over a month. Because he was one of the Seventy-Eighth's best pilots, the tempo of flight operations since April 7 had not allowed any time for Dr. Lipshitz to fix the problem. The high altitude pressurization during Jerry's time in the cockpit had made the pain even worse. Now, the doctor insisted, those teeth needed to come out.

In general, Lipshitz had been watching out for the young pilot almost since Jerry's arrival on Iwo Jima. Once, on an off day of flying for Jerry back in March, the doctor ordered him to throw on his helmet, jump in a jeep and go for a ride.

"Where are we going?" Jerry queried, as the green, open-air Army vehicle rumbled along the bumpy, primitive island road to the south, driving toward the rising outline of Mount Surabachi.

"To a Seder, Yellin."

"A Seder?"

"It's Passover."

The doc was right. It was Passover, which that year began on March 28, two days after the Banzai Massacre, and ended on April 5, two days before the first Empire Mission.

On arriving at their destination near the base of the mountain, Jerry and the doctor found Marines, low in foxholes, celebrating the Seder. The feast had been coordinated by U.S. Navy chaplains, with one of the chaplains leading the Seder in Hebrew. Though Jerry was not a practicing Jew, the experience moved him nonetheless. It also was a powerful statement from the U.S. military, that it would go to such lengths to preserve religious freedom and liberty for its Marines, sailors, and soldiers in a war-torn purgatory far from home.[1] Enjoying the short ceremony together also helped forge a bond between doctor and patient—one, however, that now was working against Jerry and his desire to fly the June 1 mission, for which he'd already been selected and which would be the granddaddy of all missions to date.

But a pilot had to be cleared medically to fly, and even the best fighter pilot couldn't fly unless okayed by the flight surgeon. Lipshitz refused to sign off on Jerry's health until he could take care of the young captain's teeth. Jerry was medically grounded for the Osaka mission; his friend and wingman Danny Mathis, who'd initially been left off the mission due to lack of experience, was scheduled to fly the *Dorrie R* in Jerry's place.

The situation upset Jerry for two reasons: he was disappointed at being left behind, but he also feared for his friend. Just one year ago, Danny had been finishing up an agriculture degree at Clemson. He was a good, promising young pilot, but by no means an experienced one, despite the fact he'd helped Jerry shoot down that Japanese aircraft only the day before. Jerry, always protective of the men who'd been his wingmen, wanted to fly the mission if for no other reason than to make sure Danny and another friend, Phil Schlamberg, would be okay. He'd already seen too many of his friends die; Fred White's passing just a few days earlier was still fresh in his memory. Jerry didn't want to lose anyone else.

But perhaps, over here, that was too much to ask.

■ ■ ■

June 1, 1945, marked the largest assault yet against Japan by the P-51 force based on Iwo Jima. All three P-51 groups—the Fifteenth, Twenty-First, and recently arrived 506th—had been assembled for the first time to escort approximately 450 B-29s on a fire-bombing raid to Osaka, an industrial city in the enemy's homeland. It was a big day, in particular, for the 506th, who, as the new kids on the block in Iwo Jima, would get a chance to prove their worth to the war effort. The three squadrons of the 506th would be led into battle by Deputy Group Commander Lieutenant Colonel Harvey Jackson Scandrett, who'd already been honored with the Silver Star and flown ninety-five combat missions, which included two shoot-downs of Japanese planes.

The 506th needed an experienced leader to counteract their relative lack of experience. Back when men such as Jerry, Tapp, and Vande Hey were flying training missions with the Seventy-Eighth in Hawaii, the 506th had not yet been formed. In the fall of 1944, its future commanding officer, Colonel Bryan B. Harper, had been stationed at Page Field just three miles south of downtown Fort Myers, Florida. Harper had taken command of the training unit of the Fifty-Third Fighter Group, which required him to get young pilots equipped to go to places like England, France, and Hawaii. But while understanding the importance of his job training pilots, Harper acknowledged something didn't quite feel right about being stationed on the beautiful, sun-baked coast of Florida—with the rich and famous frolicking along the white sandy beaches just a few miles away—while his comrades were at war. He'd deployed once already to Allbrook Field in Panama, where the U.S. Army and U.S. Navy were positioned to protect the strategic Panama Canal Zone from Axis attack. Uncontested access to the canal allowed most U.S. Navy ships to cross from the Atlantic to the Pacific without having to steam through the Magellan Straits or around Cape Horn at the southern tip of South America. The Axis, however, never attacked Panama during Bryan's deployment there, and the Army transferred him back to the States without seeing action.

Now Harper, along with many of his fellow pilots from their service in the Canal Zone, was still itching to get into the fight and finish off the enemy.

His chance came as commanding officer of the newly minted 506th, activated on October 21, 1944, at nearby Lakeland Army Air Field. The 506th was one of many units rapidly formed, mobilized and then deployed into combat to increase the Americans' firepower against the enemy that had bombed Pearl Harbor. From its inception, the 506th embraced the same goal as the already established Fifteenth and Twenty-First Fighter Groups: to fly long-range missions protecting B-29s and also attack the Japanese homeland.

Under Harper's command, the 506th quickly began training for the task ahead. Flying a variety of P-51 models, the pilots assigned to this new unit practiced long-range training regimens, including cruise control techniques that would extract maximum distance from the Mustangs. They also practiced scrambles, assembly and landing procedures, escort formations, aerial gunnery and bombing practice, and an occasional dogfight.

Then, just a month after the 506th started flying, the Army Air Force produced "Document 50–100," the published training directive for "Very Long Range" operations. Fortunately, Harper had already instituted most of the training procedures required by the directive. But his group still lacked instruction in two areas required by the directive: instrument flying and rocket firing. Knowing the 506th would not be allowed to deploy without it, Harper incorporated the lessons into the final weeks of training before they headed out to San

Diego, where the aircraft carrier USS *Kalinin Bay* was waiting to carry the unit across the Pacific.

One month later, the 506th arrived in Guam. The following week, they prepared to fly their new P-51s to Tinian, where they stayed for seven more weeks, flying combat air patrols and practice missions as the U.S. Navy Seabees and Army combat engineers on Iwo Jima prepared Airfield No. 3, or North Field, for them. The time on Tinian put the 506th in the arena of war, so to speak, though not directly in the fight. When they arrived on Iwo Jima in May, they were essentially greenhorns compared to their peers already there. In fact, even when Fifteenth and Twenty-First Fighter Groups had first landed on the island themselves, they'd already carried a number of experienced combat pilots like Vande Hey, Jerry, Tapp, and Crim. By comparison, the 506th had a larger number of rookie airmen.

Their commander Scandrett, of course, was not of that number. His men thought highly of the good-natured, blonde-haired twenty-seven-year-old Seward County native, who'd gotten married and moved to Hollywood, California, before entering the Air Force. Scandrett also commanded the trust of the group commander, Colonel Harper, who planned to remain behind in Iwo Jima with General Moore for the June 1 mission.

The navigation plan, as handed down by Moore and Harper to Scandrett the night of May 3, 1945, laid out the 506th's flight orders for the impending flight to Osaka:

1. Colonel Harper, the Group Commander, to issue the takeoff order, with all planes up by 7:10 am.
2. Set course of 357 degrees (almost due north) to rendezvous point at Kitajima, a distance of 39 nautical miles. Estimated time en route to rendezvous point: 13 minutes.
3. Rendezvous at Kitajima with B-29 navigational planes by 7:27 am at altitude of 10,000 feet.

4. Protective altitudinal cover as follows: (1) 506th Fighter Group 1,000 ft. above the B-29s; (2) 21st. Fighter Group 500 ft. above the B-29s; 15th Fighter Group 500 ft. below the B-29s.
5. Rendezvous to departure point outside Kitajima.
6. Set true course 327 degrees, fly distance 620 miles at 20,000 feet altitude from departure point.
7. Estimated flight time en route: 3 hours and 3 minutes.

As planned, on June 1, shortly before seven a.m., Moore gave the order to launch. The three group commanders relayed the command to their nine squadron commanders. Lieutenant Colonel Scandrett lifted his Mustang off Airfield No. 3, as the 506th Fighter Group followed suit.

Behind them came the Fifteenth and the Twenty-First Fighter Groups launching from Airfields No. 2 and 3. Buzzing over the skies of Iwo Jima and the outlying Pacific waters, the planes climbed to the designated altitude and set their course for the initial rendezvous point off Kitajima.

In the cockpit of the *Dorrie R*, meanwhile, First Lieutenant Danny Mathis had an additional goal in mind as the planes pushed on toward their ultimate destination: he wanted to fly this mission for Jerry, grounded back on Iwo Jima. Mathis planned to take care of the *Dorrie R* like a family member and add to his shoot-down total, which he knew would make Jerry proud. This would be the Americans' first daytime strike on Osaka, which they'd hit only once before in a night raid by B-29s on March 13–14. With a population of over 3.2 million people, Osaka was the second-largest city in Japan and its major industrial city. Its principal production included shipbuilding, steel and iron, and the manufacturing of almost everything used by the Japanese military, including propellers, munitions, and ordinance. It was also a major railway and transportation center.

The first 360 miles outside of Iwo Jima provided smooth flying conditions for the Americans, with mild winds and no turbulence. But soon a huge wall of monster cumulonimbus clouds appeared ten miles in front of the lead planes. It stretched from east to west as far as the eye could see, and from the surface of the sea all the way to the heavens.

To reach Japan, the fighters would have to find a way past that front.

The big storm system that the Mustangs had flown under just two days prior still weighed on the pilots' minds. In addition to the navigational B-29s on the mission to help guide the Mustangs around (or through) bad weather, a special radio frequency had also been established for weather discussions. With this front, it was clear going around the system was a non-starter; soon, a B-29 pilot announced over the frequency that it would begin a climb over the wall of clouds in five minutes.

But that strategy presented a problem: the planes were already too close to the front to start a climb that would enable them to clear the top.

For three minutes, the Mustangs continued flying straight at the wall. A moment later, Lieutenant Colonel Jack Thomas, commanding the Fifteenth Fighter Group, warned the B-29s that if the Mustangs penetrated the cloud cover, the whole formation would rupture.

But the B-29 radioed that it had penetrated the front without difficulty and was still on course to Osaka. Then, from inside the front itself, it radioed another message: "The oranges are sweet"—a prearranged phrase signaling good weather.

What to do? The front looked menacing. To the rapidly approaching Mustangs, it seemed they were about to fly into a great white, solid wall. Not a single pilot wanted to enter the system, but they had been ordered to follow the B-29 navigational aircraft to Japan, and the B-29 had entered and reported no turbulence.

And so, seconds later, the P-51s penetrated the front by the dozens. Scandrett led the charge, followed by his squadron leaders from the 457th, 458th, and 462nd.

While the 506th pressed on, Thomas, leading the Fifteenth, still wanted nothing to do with the system, despite the B-29's reassuring message. Scanning the clouds, he spotted what appeared to be a hole in the front over to the north and led his squadrons through the opening. Tapp, Danny Mathis, Phil Schlamberg and the other pilots of the Seventy-Eighth followed their leader into the gap.

Within five minutes, the hole closed.

Suddenly, 184 Mustangs from the Fifteenth and 506th were trapped inside a white, blinding monster. Many pilots couldn't see other planes around them. From the cockpits, it looked like they'd flown into a blizzard.

Panic set in with many, especially the less experienced pilots of the 506th. Planes started colliding with each other; others spun out of control. The weather grew increasingly violent. Planes were knocked around by high winds, and pilots desperately battled updrafts, downdrafts, and thunderous turbulence. Chaos reigned over the radios. Some of the more experienced pilots, like Tapp, pulled back on their sticks, trying to climb out of the front. The radio became a mixture of pilots' voices demanding to know other pilots' positions, announcing that they had been struck or were losing control of their aircraft. The weather was inflicting more damage than anything the Japanese had thrown at them to date.

Tapp, with Phil Schlamberg on his wing and joined by First Lieutenant Cecil Grimes, kept climbing upward. With a tight grip on his plane's stick, Tapp fought through terrific turbulence as he rose, hoping that the top of the system wasn't above the Mustang's maximum ceiling.

A few other experienced pilots tried the opposite tactic. Captain Joe Brunette of the Forty-Seventh Fighter Squadron started descending, hoping to find the bottom of the front. Lieutenant Bob Scamara, Brunette's squadron mate from the Forty-Seventh, at first tried climbing, attempting, like Tapp, to locate the top of the system. But when he found nothing but clouds, winds and more turbulence, Scamara changed his mind, reversed course, and started to descend.

Meanwhile, with the situation growing more disastrous, General Moore, who had been monitoring radio traffic about the weather conditions, issued an order to the entire fleet: "All planes. Abort mission and return to base." But the chaotic radio traffic inside the storm and radio interference from the storm itself ensured the abort order never reached the pilots.

Inside Tapp's cockpit, as he continued to climb by instruments, he watched his altimeter rise.

Twenty-one thousand, five hundred...

Twenty-two thousand...

Twenty-two thousand, five hundred...

Surely this front didn't reach all the way into outer space.

Finally, at twenty-three thousand feet...*blue skies!* Once again, the ace had beaten the odds, and he'd also saved two of his fellow pilots who'd followed him up to the clearing.

Brunette, meanwhile, struck similar luck with his course of action. He'd kept descending toward the ocean, hoping the storm didn't reach all the way down to the water's surface. At four thousand feet, he broke out into the open. He'd been followed by Second Lieutenant Eric Hutchison. Now, separated from their squadron, the pair found several stray fighters from the Seventy-Eighth and teamed with them as they continued flying south under the front.

Scamara, who'd tried ascending before descending, was still trapped in the white monster. Even when his altimeter clocked under four thousand feet, there was nothing but dense, white space surrounding the cockpit.

Perhaps there was no way out of this.

Perhaps he would descend his Mustang all the way down to the Pacific.

Thirty-eight hundred...

Thirty-five hundred...

Thirty-one hundred...

At three thousand feet, a clearing finally broke below, giving Scamara enough airspace to operate between the bottom of the clouds and the ocean. The pilot reset his course for Japan.

Many other American pilots that day were not so lucky.

By mid-afternoon, it was apparent the Seventh Fighter Command had suffered its most devastating loss since Pearl Harbor. A total of twenty-seven pilots had vanished, their planes at the bottom of the sea. The 506th had been the hardest hit fighter group.

Moore dispatched rescue planes to go search the seas for pilots who may have bailed out. Miraculously, air-sea rescue units spotted two additional pilots from the 506th in life rafts and battling horrid weather conditions. A submarine was dispatched to rescue the two stranded Americans.

But by sundown on June 1, a pervasive sadness set in among the survivors of the afternoon's tragedy. Scandrett had been killed, along with his second-in-command, Captain Edmund M. Crenshaw. Of the twenty-seven pilots lost overall, only two had been from the Seventy-Eighth, which had some of the most experienced pilots on Iwo Jima. One of the Seventy-Eighth's casualties had been First Lieutenant Jack Nelson of Oklahoma.

The other was Danny Mathis. He'd died just two days before his twenty-third birthday.

Reports came back to Jerry that the *Dorrie R* had been involved in a mid-air collision inside the storm and had plunged out of control down through the clouds. Slowly, the young pilot processed the loss of his friend and his plane on one devastating mission.

Torment set in. If he'd been able to make that flight, Danny would likely still be safe on Iwo Jima. Jerry had gone into the service straight out of high school; he'd been flying fighter planes while Danny was at Clemson. He felt instinctively he could have climbed out of the weather front. Now, questions would follow him for the rest of his life: *What if? What if he'd been flying instead of Danny—would his friend still be alive?*

As Jerry wrestled with his own queries, more arose among other fighter pilots about the failed mission. Why did the B-29 navigators lead them into such deplorable weather? Why hadn't they diverted, as Colonel Thomas requested? Why the bad communication between the B-29 navigators and the P-51s?

An investigation followed. General Hap Arnold, chief of the Army Air Force, arrived on Iwo Jima to help lead it. But as it often happened in the military, there was a finding of no fault. To Jerry, meanwhile, the reality was already as bleak as possible: his friend was never coming back.

CHAPTER 17

Five Hours over Chichi Jima

July 3, 1945

On July 3, 1945, the day before the United States' 169th birthday, there was no celebration on war-torn Iwo Jima. A little over a month had passed since Danny's death, yet the sting had not subsided for Jerry. It was hard to feel festive anyway, knowing the day might be your last on earth, or your buddy's last.

They weren't the only ones troubled that July 4 eve. Back in the States, a handful of American scientists were carrying the weight of the world on their shoulders. One of those scientists was physicist Leo Szilard, who had worked closely with Albert Einstein on the concept of nuclear physics and who had been credited with discovering a nuclear chain reaction. Szilard was working on a top-secret assignment known as "The Manhattan Project," started in 1942 to produce the first atomic bomb. American scientists had worked round the clock on the weapon out of fear that the Nazis would build it first and use it during the war. The U.S. program was first based in Manhattan, New York (hence, the project's name), but most of the work was soon transferred to Oak Ridge, Tennessee, while the testing facility was established in Los Alamos, New Mexico.

But after helping invent the bomb, Szilard had become afraid of its use. He disbelieved the military's assurance that it would be used only against military targets, and he also worried that its great destructive power, even if aimed directly at such targets, would consume far more than the targets alone. To Szilard, warning against the bomb's use became a moral imperative; he believed that he and his fellow scientists, if they did not speak up, would be viewed no differently than Nazi exterminators in the court of world opinion. Perhaps they would even be treated in the same vein as Nazi war criminals and face trial with possible execution.

Thus concerned, Szilard circulated a letter and petition among several scientists working with him on the project. The documents ultimately asked President Truman not to use the bomb against the Japanese. The petition's first version, passed about on the eve of Independence Day in 1945, was more strongly-worded than later versions and concluded that atomic bombs would become "a means for the ruthless annihilation of cities."

Meanwhile, half a world away, Jerry and his fellow pilots continued prosecuting an air war that seemed to have no end in sight. After the disastrous fiasco of June 1, the command had lost two pilots the rest of the month, neither in Jerry's squadron. One of these was First Lieutenant John V. Scanlan of Kentucky, a member of the Forty-Seventh, whose plane had taken fire from a Japanese Zero. Scanlan bailed out, and, soon after landing, was taken in by a group of Japanese ladies, who sheltered him in safety. Eventually, however, a young, angry mob surrounded the women and demanded Scanlan be turned over to them. The women complied, and the mob murdered him. Earlier that month, Second Lieutenant Arthur Zellweger of the Seventy-Second had been killed over Chichi Jima by antiaircraft fire while strafing the enemy airstrip.

The morning of July 3, from the cockpit of his new plane, the *Dorrie R II*, Jerry had led a squadron of eight P-51s to Chichi Jima.

Over the past four months, the Americans had been consistent about firing on the airfield there every few days, trying to keep it inoperable. Each time they struck, however, the Japanese would patch it up just enough to make it functional. And an operational Japanese airfield, left unchecked and so close to Iwo Jima, could be catastrophic to the Army's air operations there. Thus, no matter what the secondary target was for American pilots at Chichi Jima—and there were always secondary targets—the airfield got hit first. It was also part of a strategy to keep Japanese fighter planes out of the sky during the American attacks. Facing their antiaircraft fire was dangerous enough, and the repetitive pattern of *attack, repair, attack*, meant that the Japanese weren't going to be surprised when the Mustangs arrived. They would be waiting and ready to deliver heavy antiaircraft fire, which made the close-in attack runs by the P-51s extremely dangerous propositions.

Led by Jerry, the eight Mustangs arrived on time: eight a.m. His wingman that day was another good friend, Richard Henry Schroeppel, known to his squadron mates as Dick. Like Jerry, Dick hailed from New Jersey, about twenty miles from the little house on Bond Street where Jerry had grown up. Born on December 23, 1923, Dick was only fifty-four days older than Jerry, whose birthday fell on February 15, 1924. Given their Jersey roots and closeness in age, the two developed a special bond and were often discussed by their fellow pilots as if they were a single package. Around the squadron, they were affectionately known as "Joiseyites."

With the early-morning sun glistening off the waters to the east, the American planes circled the airspace of Chichi Jima to feel out their targets. On this mission, the secondary target was shipping in Futami Harbor. First, as usual, came the airfield.

Banking the *Dorrie R II* and with Dick Schroeppel on his wing, Jerry led the P-51s into attack formation. He began his descent from eight thousand feet, angling down at the airfield, his eyes focused on the target. Bullets and tracers from Japanese antiaircraft fire whizzed past, inches from his glass cockpit.

Jerry squeezed down on the trigger of the Mustang's .50-caliber guns. Six streams of lead shot out from his plane and rushed to the earth, tearing up everything in their path. He kept his guns firing, strafing the length of the airfield and sending plumes of smoke and dust into the air.

He pulled up over the harbor as Dick followed him in for a second round. But when Jerry turned around, he saw Dick's plane in flames. The aircraft had been struck by the torrid stream of Japanese bullets flying up from the ground.

Dick was at low altitude, which meant he didn't have much time to bail. Yet somehow, he managed to pull up and jump out as the burning plane shot out over the harbor.

Jerry circled around again, keeping his eye on his friend as he floated down, hanging at the bottom of his parachute over enemy territory. Jerry radioed for help, then circled again, still monitoring Dick's descent. Dick was losing control of the parachute, but he didn't have far to drop. His Mustang, meanwhile, still burning and smoking, flew out to sea and soon crashed in the ocean near the shoreline, where rocks protruded out of the water. Jerry noted his chronometer. It was 10:06 a.m. when Dick's plane went down.

Dick, having landed safely, quickly cut the chute, then removed his C-2 life raft pack away from the chute and stripped down to his skivvies. He got his life raft inflated and pushed it out into the surf. Every pilot watching from overhead knew that Dick's only chance for survival was to paddle like hell and move as far as possible away from the shore before the Japanese could get their hands on him. Jerry watched as Dick jumped into the raft and started paddling furiously with his hands against the raging surf.

But as Dick pushed his raft out farther, Japanese gun batteries from the shore opened fire, their bullets splashing in the water all around the downed American pilot.

Jerry's call for help over the radio, meanwhile, had not gone unnoticed. The U.S. Navy already had a PBY Catalina—capable of

landing in the sea—patrolling the area. Iwo Jima also radioed that a
B-17 rescue plane was on the way to drop a larger boat for Dick to
use. And a P-51 squadron headed for Japan had diverted toward
Chichi Jima to relieve Jerry's squadron. Within minutes, more firepower would be arriving.

Jerry was still circling overhead, and as the Japanese opened fire
on Dick, he pushed down on his throttle, broke out of his orbit, and
opened fire in the direction of the gunfire. Other members of the
squadron followed suit, pouring bullets down on the rocky coast,
trying to provide cover for Dick.

The P-51 fire seemed to slow down the enemy onslaught for a
moment, but the Japanese were everywhere, firing from unseen places
in the crevices of the rocks. In fact, the source of the bullets fired at
Dick wasn't always clear.

But Dick was still alive and managed to paddle out a good distance from shore. He struggled, however, to fight the strong, inbound
currents. Japanese machine-gun fire and now mortar fire splashed all
around him. He tried staying low to dodge the onslaught while his
friends in the sky continued to pound the shore.

For two hours, a furious battle ensued, with P-51 Mustangs
circling and firing into the beaches and cliffs of Chichi Jima, and
Japanese infantry ducking behind rocks, then coming out to take
shots at Dick.

Jerry's squadron began running low on fuel. With the rest of his
men, Jerry was forced to begin a return flight to Iwo Jima as Dick
remained in the water below. More fighters, however, had arrived to
provide air support. In fact, some forty P-51s were now buzzing
through the air, trying like hell to save their comrade.

Around noon, the wide wingspan of a B-17 bomber, known as a
"Flying Dutchman," appeared from the south. Modified for long-
range search and rescue missions over the ocean, these particular
B-17s carried an A-1 Higgins lifeboat under their fuselage to rescue
downed pilots. Twenty-seven feet long and weighing thirty-three

hundred pounds, these lifeboats could be dropped by parachute from the B-17s to air crews floating in the Pacific. The boats were made of laminated mahogany with twenty waterproof internal compartments, rendering them unsinkable if swamped or overturned. The lifeboat was also supplied with sufficient water, clothing and food for up to twelve men to last twenty days on the ocean. There was even a survival radio with a kite for an antenna, small sails, and two small engines that would propel the boat up to eight miles per hour, with enough fuel to cruise fifteen hundred miles. If the B-17 could drop the boat, and if Dick could manage to get aboard, hopefully he could crank the engines and at least get out of range of Japanese fire, giving the U.S. Navy a solid chance to pluck him from the water.

As the B-17 approached, however, a weary Dick had been pushed by strong swells up against a wall of rocks protruding from the water. But those rocks—at least for the time being—protected him from the sight of Japanese gunners and their bullets.

P-51 pilots circling overhead kept an eye on Dick and reported that he appeared exhausted.

As the B-17 moved into the area, a P-51 flew out to escort the bomber in and provide protection against Japanese shore fire coming from Chichijma. Other P-51s stepped up, again pouring fire onto the coasts and cliffs to provide cover for the B-17 to work. The pilot of the B-17, First Lieutenant Claude L. Bodin Jr., passed low over the bay, trying to get a visual on Dick. But Dick was still up against the rock barrier, and Bodin did not see him on the first round.

More Mustangs arrived on the scene, filling the air like a swarm of hornets. As the Mustangs and the Japanese continued to exchange fire, the big B-17 made another pass over the water, trying to locate the downed flyer among the rocks just offshore. This time, Dick had managed to release a dye marker into the water. Bodin got a visual on Dick and maneuvered into position to launch the lifeboat. At 12:40 p.m., with the Mustangs fending off heavy Japanese fire, Bodin pulled the release lever. The boat dropped from the underbelly of the B-17, and three parachutes deployed. Dangling below them, the Higgins floated down to the ocean, then splashed a hundred yards or so out at sea, south of the protective rocks under which Dick was taking cover.

It was now or never for the young pilot.

Dick hesitated for a second, then jumped into the surf and started swimming toward the floating lifeboat. With incoming swells crashing into his face and Japanese bullets flying at him from behind, he swam hard, as his fellow pilots kept up the battle for his life from overhead.

A moment later, he broke out of the swells and made it to the boat, pulling himself up and over the side, which set off a torrent of furious Japanese machine-gun fire into the craft. From the air, Dick appeared to be lying still in the bottom of the boat.

His countrymen were uncertain: Had he been hit? Or was he lying low to stay below Japanese bullets?

Meanwhile, the U.S. Army OA-10 Catalina, the Army's version of the Navy's famous "Flying Boat," was on patrol a few miles out and had been monitoring the radio traffic about the ongoing rescue efforts. The Catalina had a flying boat hull and was capable of landing in water. The plane's pilot, twenty-one-year-old Captain Robert B. Richardson of Irvine, Kentucky, radioed in and announced that he had a flight surgeon on board. Base command told Richardson to "land at your own discretion."

Between the rocks and reefs all around the Higgins boat, the rough swells and Japanese bullets and mortars still flying in, it was practically a suicide mission. But Richardson and his men were in agreement. They would sacrifice their lives, if necessary, to save a fellow countryman—one they did not even know—if at all possible.

"We're going in," Richardson announced.

As the Catalina approached Chichi Jima, a flight of Mustangs that had been attacking the island flew out to the Catalina to provide cover. Ten of those Mustangs then accompanied it into the battle zone.

With the shore and cliffs rapidly approaching through the wind-shield of the cockpit, Richardson turned the Catalina for a water-landing attempt. Exposing himself to direct Japanese gunfire, the flight surgeon aboard the aircraft entered the glass-bubble, gun-mount "blister" on the fuselage, hoping to get a look at Dick. Richardson started a landing run, his eyes on the Higgins boat holding the downed pilot. The pilot came in too low on the attempt, however, and the Catalina bounced along the water near the lifeboat, which was about a hundred yards offshore.

The pilot pulled up, circled around and tried again. This time, he succeeded. The Catalina floated in the water. With bullets splashing all around, Richardson idled the Catalina over towards the lifeboat, coming so close that the pontoon scraped against its hull.

The flight surgeon looked down from the glass bubble into the boat. Dick was riddled with bullet holes in the head, chest, and leg. The body was not salvageable.

Now, at least, they knew. Dick was gone.

It was time to get out of there, lest Richardson and his crewmen also fall victim to the Japanese. With the Mustangs providing cover, Richardson pushed the throttle forward, and the Catalina cut through the water, but it was now under heavy fire. Mortars splashed in the sea around the plane, spraying water over the outside of the cockpit. Neither Richardson nor his co-pilot could see anything but the water being thrown up against their windshield. It would be a miracle if Richardson were able to get the plane airborne.

He pushed down on the throttle.

More mortar fire. More spraying water. The Catalina picked up speed. More mortar fire. Richardson could still see little—except the spray of bullets trying to end his life. A few seconds later, he felt the nose of the Catalina lift up, and the wind set under the flaps of his wings. The angry spraying water was gone. A blue, mid-day sky dominated his view.

As Richardson put the Catalina into a steep climb, taking it far outside the reach of the Japanese shore batteries on Chichi Jima, word spread over the pilots' radios of Dick's death. The Seventy-Eighth had lost another good man.

Filled with grief, the pilots of the P-51s circled overhead, looking down at their fallen comrade in the bottom of the boat. It was their brief chance to say goodbye. As painful as this next step would be, they had no choice, for there was one thing they knew for sure: hell would freeze over before they let the lifeless body in the boat fall into the hands of the Japanese.

The pilots circled back in attack formation and made a run at the Higgins boat. A barrage of machine gun fire and rockets blew the craft out of the water and sunk it to the bottom.

Now, at least, their friend's body would never be cannibalized by the enemy.

Back at Iwo Jima, word reached Jerry about Dick's death. The news took his breath away. The twenty-one-year-old had lost yet another dear friend.

How many daggers could a single heart take?

CHAPTER 18

Heartbreak over Tokyo

July 8, 1945

The institution of war knows no patience, nor compassion. As before, Jerry had little time to mourn the loss of a close friend. The war went on, refusing to pause for grief. At best, its incessant demands might offer a tonic for dealing with it.

By July 8, the young pilot was in the air again. The Fifteenth Fighter Group was flying that day with the Twenty-First on a mission over Tokyo. At first, Jerry hadn't known many of the pilots from that unit; they'd tended to congregate at Airfield No. 2 and keep to themselves. But after the Banzai attack, that began to change; some of the Fifteenth's more experienced airmen—including a few of the Seventy-Eighth's better pilots—had been transferred to the Twenty-First to fill the places of those injured or killed. One of those transferred was Captain Al Sherren.

Still, something didn't seem right about Al being anywhere but the Seventy-Eighth. Al was one of Jerry's best friends in the Army; they'd met in Phoenix in 1942, when they were both new aviation cadets at Luke Field. They went through flight school together and

137

afterwards had been part of the same training class in Haliewa, Oahu, reporting fresh out of flight school in October of 1943. Along with Bob Roseberry and Bob Ruby—who, like Al, were from Iowa—the quartet formed a special bond as the first cadets of the Seventy-Eighth to arrive at Haliewa. Upon reporting, they were told they would receive at least fifty hours of training before being shipped out to a combat zone.

Their first lessons were in the old P-40 (the P-51 had yet to be developed). Jerry had been assigned to the wing of Captain Vic Mollan in Jim Tapp's flight, and, while American forces were challenging the Japanese in the Makin Islands, Jerry and the Iowa boys practiced, practiced, and practiced some more, flying simulated combat drills in the air, mimicking strafing targets on the ground, dive-bombing targets in the sea, and mastering the art of dog-fighting.

Together, the quartet lived through the first loss of a comrade before ever entering a war zone: that of their first squadron commander, Major Bill Southerland, in a mid-air collision.

The following April, Lieutenant Ed Green, a young pilot from Massachusetts who had become good friends with Jerry, lost control of his new P-47 Thunderbolt during a training exercise. Green had played first base on the squadron's softball team and was in many respects a leader among his peers. But the new P-47 he flew was much faster than the P-40 and thus more prone to go into a flat spin. The last words anyone ever heard Ed say came over his radio as he flew over the Pacific off the cost of Hawaii: "Mayday! Mayday! I'm in a flat spin! I can't get out." They never found Ed's body, nor even an oil slick from the plane.

Unfortunately, Ed wasn't the only pilot to die during training exercises off Hawaii. There was Lieutenant Howard Edmonson, the pilot who earlier had collided with Southerland, and Lieutenant Bob Ferris, who died one month before Christmas Day, 1944, when the P-51 he was piloting in a demonstration flight literally disintegrated before Jerry's eyes over Bellows Field in Hawaii, the result of high-speed maneuvering gone awry. Like Green, Ferris' body was never found. Fellow pilot John Lindner was killed two months later in a maneuver similar to the one Ferris had tried to execute. Lindner started a steep dive over Bellows Field, then tried to pull up too quickly. The harsh G-forces against the aircraft tore the wings off the fuselage. Within seconds, John was dead. This was on January 13, 1945, just a few days before the Seventy-Eighth shipped out on the *Sitkoh Bay*.

The reality of death had cemented Jerry and the Iowa boys together, even before they'd dodged a bullet from the enemy. They shipped out together on USS *Sitkoh Bay* in January of 1945 to Guam, and then to Iwo Jima, where they fought the Japanese together.

At five-foot-six-inches tall, with brown hair and blue eyes, Al wasn't a physically imposing officer. One of the first things he and Jerry bonded over was their love of cigarettes. During the war, cigarettes became a popular pastime with many of the pilots. Al was a Lucky Strikes guy; Jerry preferred Chesterfields. Their differing taste generated plenty of friendly banter, especially when one ran out of cigarettes and the other remained stocked. Sometimes, when Al had used up the last of his "Luckies" and Jerry tossed him a pack of Chesterfields as a temporary holdover, Al lit one and smoked it while feigning disgust. Other times, he laughed, pulled out a single Chesterfield from the pack, studied it as if contemplating whether to light it or not, then threw it on the ground and stomped on it, his aficionado tastes too sublime to stoop to a "Chester" even at the moment. Al was a funny guy, a "life-of-the-party" type, and often clowned around. Sometimes, he'd switch his cap around backwards and mimic a German submarine officer. The guys always got a kick out of that routine. But he could also be persuasive. Eventually, he even convinced Jerry to "move up" to the Luckies.

Al, along with Jerry, was part of today's strike force over Tokyo. None of the missions flown from Iwo Jima to Japan that July were escort missions, which meant the P-51s would not be rendezvousing with B-29s. Rather, the Mustangs would be flying on their own, designated to attack targets of opportunity. The Mustangs' focus this time was the Hyakurigahara and Tokorozawa Airfields in the Tokyo area. Hyakurigahara was one of the major garrison headquarters of Japan's 721st Naval Air Group, which had been organized to launch kamikaze attacks against the U.S. Navy and other American targets. Tokorozawa, meanwhile, was the site of Japan's first military airfield and its air service academy. It was considered a strategic fighter base during the war. Both of these airbases needed to be taken out, or at least damaged, to negate their operational effectiveness. The Mustangs planned to hit them on repeated strafing and bombing attacks, render them non-operational, and return to base.

Except for some squalls the P-51s had to maneuver around about 350 miles out of Iwo Jima, the first leg of the 1,645-mile round-trip flight went smoothly. On the initial pass over the Hyakurigahara Airfield, the Forty-Seventh Fighter Squadron flew high cover for the pilots of the Seventy-Eighth. From eleven thousand feet, Jerry started a steep dive toward the target, attacking from east to west. In their pre-flight briefing, the pilots had seen two antiaircraft guns positioned on the airfield that they marked for attack. But on their first pass, the guns were not spotted. Perhaps the Japanese had moved them out of view to prevent their becoming targets.

However, a number of dummy aircraft and biplanes that were being used as decoys were spotted along the side and edges of the field as Jerry began his first strafing run, firing all along the runway and into side buildings. Other pilots of the Seventy-Eighth followed suit, shooting at the airfield with devastating fury. Because of the steep angle of attack, however, not all the pilots fired on this initial pass. The squadron pulled up, regrouped, and prepared to attack again.

On the second run, when the pilots had a better chance to eyeball the target area, they spotted a number of Japanese warplanes on the ground under camouflaged netting and parked inside of three-sided concrete revetments. Several other planes were hidden northwest of the airfield, also well-camouflaged under trees and farm buildings. Intense antiaircraft fire started rising up from buildings to the northwest of the airfield. Japanese antiaircraft fire at point-blank range was often more lethal than the Japanese fighter planes in mid-air, and the enemy had placed such firepower all around the area where they'd hidden their aircraft.

Flying into the teeth of the enemy's fire, Jerry lowered the fighter into an attack run and opened repeatedly on the targets. As the Seventy-Eighth continued its work, one of the buildings alongside the airfield burst in flames. The Japanese were firing from a number of concrete buildings surrounding the airfield and also from a ridge south of the building area, but the Seventy-Eighth's return fire proved effective. Two Japanese planes on the south side of the field ignited.

With the Forty-Seventh still flying cover overhead, the Seventy-Eighth cleared out to make way for an attack pass by the Forty-Fifth Fighter Squadron, Al Sherren's new group. Jerry was among those that pulled up and circled around as the Forty-Fifth started their run.

What came next would haunt him for the rest of his life.

A voice came over the squadron's emergency radio frequency: *"Mayday! Mayday! I'm hit and I can't see!"*

It was Al Sherren. Those were the last words he uttered.

Later, the Waterloo Courier—Al's hometown paper—quoted details from the Army's press release describing the young pilot's cause of death: "Sherren was injured by enemy gunfire during a strafing run and, after radioing his flight commander that he had sustained head injury and could not see, headed for base and was believed to have crashed in the Pacific Ocean."

Jerry's flight back to Iwo Jima that Sunday afternoon was the hardest he'd made to date. And he landed to more bad news: his tentmate, Bob Carr, had been shot down somewhere over Tokyo. No one had heard any distress calls from Carr, but his plane had disappeared.

Jerry taxied the *Dorrie R II* to a stop, powered down and got out. Personal grief struck him like no time prior in this monstrous war.

Since June, death had come in quick waves—Danny Mathis, Dick Schroeppel, now Sherren and Carr. No mission the young pilot had ever flown would be as hard as the task now awaiting him: to pack the clothes of Al Sherren and Bob Carr, put them in footlockers, and ship them home to their families.

CHAPTER 19

The Blazing Winds of August

Tinian Island—The Marianas

At 2:45 a.m. on August 6, 1945, a solitary B-29 bomber lifted off the end of the North Field runway on Tinian Island.

The aircraft nosed upward under a moonless night, angling toward the Milky Way. The galaxy painted a great sparkling display across the black heavens, while a dome of stars stretched from horizon to horizon, down to the dark waters of the ocean. The twelve men aboard the aircraft watched the breathtaking display in stunned silence.

The plane climbed just over five thousand feet above the water, a relatively low altitude for a B-29. Up near the cockpit, Captain Theodore "Dutch" Van Kirk, the twenty-four-year-old navigator of the bomber that less than twenty-four hours ago had been named the *Enola Gay,* plotted his course and relayed coordinates to the plane's pilot, thirty-year-old Colonel Paul Tibbets. In accordance with Operation Order 35, which had been issued by the 509th Composite Group and signed by Major James I. Hopkins Jr., only the day before, the *Enola Gay* would first fly north towards the airspace over Iwo Jima, then rendezvous with two other bombers in the air. The trio of planes would next ascend to thirty-one thousand feet over Iwo Jima to take themselves out of range of enemy fighters and antiaircraft fire, after which they would re-calibrate their course for their ultimate destination: Japan. Their mission that night had been personally ordered by their commander in chief, Harry S. Truman, who'd succeeded Franklin Delano Roosevelt in the U.S. presidency. And the arguments that had been made the month prior by Leo Szilard and other physicists on the Manhattan Project had failed: the atomic bomb was going to be unleashed on the enemy.

Except for the sonorous roar of the bomber's four engines, the first three hours of the flight were marked by silence, as the crew contemplated its mission. They reached Iwo Jima just as the sun began to rise, with the distinctive "pork chop" outline in the water coming into the view below them.

Above Iwo Jima, two other B-29s were circling as they awaited the *Enola Gay*. One B-29 named *The Great Artiste*, under the command of Major Charles W. Sweeny, would serve as an observation aircraft for the mission. It carried, in addition to its crew, three civilian members of Project Alberta, part of the top-secret Manhattan Project. On board were special instruments for blast measurement to collect data and relay information about the weapon that would be dropped from the bomb bay of the *Enola Gay*. As for Sweeny himself, if he survived this mission, he had another within the next few days just like it, in the lead plane called the *Bockscar* over the city of Nagasaki.

The third B-29 to join the group bore a codename of *Victor 91* and was later renamed *Necessary Evil*. Commanded by twenty-six-year-old Captain George W. Marquardt, *Necessary Evil* was tasked with the job of photographing the events of the mission. The images Marquardt captured that day would later ensure his place in the annals of history.

Once over Iwo Jima, the planes, as planned, climbed to thirty-one thousand feet, maneuvered into a three-plane battle formation, and set their course for Japan. Weather patterns appeared clear for the final leg of the flight.

Now it was just a matter of time.

Three hours later, the planes crossed into Japanese airspace. With the sun shining off their gray-silver wings, they would have been visible from the ground some five miles below. Yet they had arrived over Japanese airspace seemingly unnoticed. The Japanese, for their part, did not seem worried about a very small number of random bombers flying so far overhead. Their cities had been blasted by mighty waves of three hundred and four hundred bombers coming at once, with another hundred P-51s flying alongside. Besides, those attacks had come from much lower altitudes. What damage could a measly trio of planes, flying so high without any fighter coverage, possibly cause? The Americans had already learned that bombs dropped from five miles in the sky were not reliable and oftentimes did not damage their target from that high up. If these planes came down low enough to drop bombs, and without fighter cover, the Japanese air force would shoot them down.

As the *Enola Gay* flew over the Japanese island of Shikoku toward Hiroshima, the plane's bombardier, Major Tom Ferebee, moved into the nose section of the plane, where the large, glass bubble afforded him a panoramic view of the Japanese coastline. A moment later, he called out:

"I got it!"

He turned to the plane's navigator for a second opinion.

Van Kirk moved up into the nose section of the *Enola Gay* and confirmed that Ferebee had spotted the target area: the Aioi Bridge, designated as ground zero.

As the *Enola Gay* approached Hiroshima at thirty-one thousand feet, Tibbets, speaking through a microphone to the rest of his crew, initialed a countdown of T-minus three minutes.

Ferebee had crawled back into the bomb bay of the *Enola Gay*, his heart pounding as Tibbets counted down. With the bomber's four powerful engines humming in a monotone roar, they crossed over the borders of Hiroshima and closed in on the Aioi Bridge.

The nine-thousand-pound weapon the crew was about to drop had never been used in war before. The men knew little about what it would do, or even if it would detonate. They did know, however, that one like it had been tested in the American desert in New Mexico. The blast from that test, they were told, was a thousand times brighter than the sun itself and created powerful winds that could be felt miles away. The test had produced a mushroom cloud that climbed forty thousand feet into the sky, almost ten thousand feet above the *Enola Gay*'s current position. The shockwave from that bomb had also been felt ten miles from the explosion. People up to sixty miles away at Alamogordo Army Air Field had been able to see the light from the explosion.

It all meant not a single man aboard the *Enola Gay* knew whether they would survive if the bomb they dropped actually detonated. Would a great fireball rise up and engulf the aircraft?

Would winds and turbulence from the blast send the bomber spinning out of control? Every man aboard had volunteered for the mission, however, and each was prepared to give his life to help force an end to this war.

Meanwhile, from the cockpit, Tibbets continued counting down:

"Eight."

"Seven."

"Six."

"Five."

"Four."

"Three."

"Two."

"One."

"Zero."

It was 8:15:17 a.m.

Ferebee pushed a lever in the bomb bay and made sure an automatic system he'd activated seconds earlier had functioned. He watched as the single, nine-thousand-pound bomb, nicknamed "Little Boy," turned nose-down and dropped through the sky toward its target, Aioi Bridge, which Ferebee had originally selected back in the States from aerial photographs.

As the bomb fell, the nose of the *Enola Gay* lurched upward and Tibbets put the plane into a quick 160-degree turn, a desperate maneuver to get the aircraft as far away as possible from the impending blast. Tibbets had practiced this maneuver on multiple occasions; now, he needed to execute it to perfection.

As he turned the aircraft and went full throttle, the crew awaited the explosion. Some thought the bomb might have been a dud. Van Kirk later reported, "Everyone was counting, 'One thousand one, one thousand two...'"

The bomb fell for a total of forty-three seconds.

Then, suddenly, a great, blinding light filled the *Enola Gay*'s cabin. Van Kirk later described it as a "photographer's bulb going off." Tibbets reported it "lit up the sky" and seemed to have "a bluish hue." Seconds later, a great shock wave struck the *Enola Gay*. The plane jumped and made a frightening noise like the sound of sheet metal snapping.

The men held their breath. For a moment, it seemed the bomber would disintegrate in the sky. A second wave hit the plane a moment later. But it held together.

Crew members looked out at where the city of Hiroshima had been. The area was covered with smoke, dust, and dirt, and looked like a pot of black, boiling tar as fires raged on its edge. Tibbets turned and flew in an arc from the northeast to the southeast of the disintegrating city. The mushroom cloud climbed into the sky, its stem full of tumbling debris, and rising far above the *Enola Gay*'s current altitude of twenty-six thousand feet. The men were relieved that the bomber had not been damaged.

It was time to get out of Japan.

Moments later, the *Enola Gay* was back over the Pacific, headed south toward Tinian.

CHAPTER 20

Jerry Hears the News

August 6, 1945

Jerry looked down at the familiar, pork chop-shaped island, with the small mountain rising at the far-right end of it, as he made his final turn out over the water and lined up with the airfield stretching from the base of Mount Suribachi. From his vantage point, the Quonset huts along the coast of the island looked smaller than postage stamps, and the sea of P-51 fighters and Army jeeps parked along the side of the airfield appeared even smaller. Iwo Jima would never look like home. But at least there was a degree of comfort knowing that friends and fellow countrymen were there, and the island was—at least for the time being—relatively safe from imminent Japanese attack.

It was the afternoon of August 6, 1945, and the Seventy-Eighth was returning from a strafing mission over Tokyo, during which Jerry had attacked several strategic airfields. There had been no casualties among the men of the Seventy-Eighth that day, for which Jerry was grateful. But the Fifteenth Fighter Group had suffered one; First Lieutenant Howard Weaver of the Forty-Seventh would never return home. It was one loss out of the entire group, but still one too many. And after Jerry's hellish July, he knew all too well the pain his brothers in the Forty-Seventh were about to feel.

With the nose of his aircraft lined up with the end of the runway, Jerry brought the *Dorrie R II* in for landing, flaring up on the nose as he felt the wheels touch the ground. Just as he throttled down the *Dorrie R II*, and even before the plane's propeller stopped spinning, he saw one of his buddies, Phil Maher, who had been Jim Tapp's go-to wingman, running toward the plane and waving his arms. Phil then jumped up on one of the wings and started shouting:

"It's over, it's over! We dropped one bomb, wiped out a city, no more missions, it's over!"

Jerry looked down from the cockpit, confused. No one had briefed the Seventy-Eighth about any missions being flown against Japan that day except their attacks on Tokyo.

"What are you smoking, Phil?" Jerry shot back. "Whatever it is, I want some."

He soon discovered, however, that Phil's excited utterances were true—at least the part about the bomb. The Twentieth Air Force had dropped a super-weapon on Hiroshima with a destructive power almost beyond imagination. At the very moment the city had been engulfed in flames, obliterated by a nuclear blast from something being called the "atom bomb," Jerry and his fellow pilots of the Seventy-Eighth had been attacking Tokyo, 420 miles away from this secret mission.

As a result of this newly deployed super-weapon, a false sense of relief swept over the Seventh Fighter Command as they learned the news. They thought Japan had been delivered its death blow and that the war was over. Rumors flew: Japan's surrender was imminent, the Seventy-Eighth would be transferred there, or they were going to be transferred to the Philippines. An even better rumor followed: they were staying together as a unit and going back to the States.

None of those rumors, of course, materialized. As devastating as the atomic bomb had been to Hiroshima, the stubborn Japanese refused to surrender.

This war was not over. Not yet, anyway.

CHAPTER 21

The Enemy Stalls

The day after the atomic bomb had been dropped on Hiroshima, the Seventh Fighter Command flew a long-range mission to Toyokawa, home to the Toyokawa Naval Arsenal. During this attack, forty-eight Mustangs from Iwo Jima escorted 135 B-29s launched from Guam, Saipan, and Tinian The American warplanes arrived over the target area at 10:13 a.m.; twelve B-29s peeled off to attack the naval arsenal, while the remaining bombers concentrated on Toyokawa's civilian population center.

Still, Japan did not surrender.

The next day, August 8, more missions were launched against the island, this time by the Twenty-First Fighter Group and the newly arrived 414th Air Group. On August 9, another solitary B-29, this one named *Bockscar*, dropped another atomic bomb. In a flash, the city of Nagasaki vanished. This bomb was even more powerful than the first dropped on Hiroshima. It set off another wave of rumors that Japan was about to surrender.

President Harry S. Truman took to the airways to deliver a blunt message to the world.

The British, Chinese, and United States Governments have given the Japanese people adequate warning of what is in store for them. We have laid down the general terms on which they can surrender. Our warning went unheeded; our terms were rejected. Since then, the Japanese have seen what our atomic bomb can do. They can foresee what it will do in the future....

Having found the bomb we have used it. We have used it against those who attacked us without warning at Pearl Harbor, against those who have starved and beaten and executed American prisoners of war, against those who have abandoned all pretense of obeying international laws of warfare. We have used it in order to shorten the agony of war, in order to save the lives of thousands and thousands of young Americans.

We shall continue to use it until we completely destroy Japan's power to make war. Only a Japanese surrender will stop us."

The president's ominous warning to Japan increased hope among the American pilots on Iwo Jima that the war would end.

Still, Japan did not capitulate the day Nagasaki was bombed.

Nor did they officially surrender the next day, nor the next, although negotiations had begun regarding the terms of a possible surrender on August 10. President Truman slowed down the frequency of the air strikes, which only fueled the surrender rumors even more. But when those talks began to break down, the Twentieth Air Force was ordered to step up the air raids again.

On August 14, at four p.m., Tapp called members of the Seventy-Eighth together at the command Quonset hut to announce a mission for the following day.

The men of the Seventy-Eighth had thought—or at least hoped—the war was over. They asked Tapp why they were going to fly the mission.

"We have to keep them honest," Tapp responded. He added that if the Japanese surrendered while the mission was in progress, the Seventh Fighter Command would radio out the code signal "UTAH." If the signal went out, the Seventy-Eighth would turn around and fly back to Iwo Jima.

At the meeting, Jerry sat next to his good friend Phil Schlamberg. During the briefing, Phil leaned over and whispered into Jerry's ear, "If I go on this mission, captain, I'm not coming back."

"What are you talking about, Phil?" Jerry gave him a curious look.

"The feeling I have," Phil mumbled.

It wasn't the first time Jerry witnessed a pilot having a premonition about his own death. Phil's comments bothered him so much that he tracked down Tapp and voiced his concern: Phil should not be flying on this mission. Jerry knew it in his gut.

Tapp, who always put his men first, was sympathetic.

"Look, Jerry," he said. "If Phil goes to see Doc Lewis, and Doc Lewis gives him a waiver, that's the only way we can excuse him from the mission." Doc Lewis was the flight surgeon for the Fifteenth Fighter Group.

Jerry, in turn, went to Phil and suggested he go see Doc Lewis.

But Phil flat-out refused.

"No," he insisted, "I'm going to fly the mission."

And that was that.

Still, Phil's premonition bothered Jerry. Frankly, Jerry felt a bit protective of him; he'd spent a bit of time with the nineteen-year-old and had gotten to know him better than most of the others on Iwo Jima did. Phil was actually the youngest of ten children in a family of Jewish-Polish immigrants. He'd been born on the lower east side of Manhattan before moving to a poor section of Coney Island in Brooklyn. The two oldest of the Schlamberg children, who were actually Phil's stepsiblings, had grown up in a different household than the eight youngest. When Phil's dad left his mom early on, these younger eight were left basically to live on welfare in their mother's small, one-bedroom Coney Island apartment. The Schlamberg kids were so poor growing up—and so hungry—that they illegally sold ice cream on the beach in the summertime to make extra money for food. Often, they were rounded up off the beach by the police and even arrested for selling without a permit. But that didn't stop the kids. Once released, they'd go back down to the beaches and sell more ice cream.

Phil, known as "Phelly," was viewed as something of a lovable pest by his older brothers and sisters, yet he was nevertheless their favorite. They were a hard-working bunch, and not just illegally selling ice cream on the beach. Five of the kids, including Phil, graduated as valedictorian from nearby Abraham Lincoln High School. Phil himself displayed many talents: along with being an academic whiz, he was an amateur musician and learned to play the harmonica well, choosing it because it was the only instrument that he could afford. Upon graduation from Abraham Lincoln with highest honors, he hoped to attend college before going into the military. However, though he'd been accepted to college, he had no money for tuition or books. His older brothers Michael and Sidney had already joined the military, with Michael in the Army and Sidney in the Army Air Force. Neither were pilots—Michael had actually been disqualified because of inner ear problems. But he'd scored well on his Army aptitude tests and became a Morse code expert assigned to the China-Burma-India Theater. When Phil later took the Army aptitude tests, his scores—including his I.Q. results—were among the highest ever recorded by the U.S. military. Based on those numbers, the Army basically offered Phil whatever job he wanted. And Phil wanted to fly fighter planes, which, until now, had proved a good choice.

It should be noted that each and every pilot who flew for the U.S. Army and the U.S. Navy in World War II volunteered to do so. The American military never forced anyone into the cockpit of an airplane during the war. Every U.S. pilot knew the risk of getting into a combat aircraft and flying into an active war zone. Both Phil and Jerry were willing to accept whatever cost each mission might exact.

The next twenty-four hours would tell.

CHAPTER 22

Over Tokyo

The Final Mission
August 15, 1945

A fighter pilot's mindset was one of the most important things he carried into battle. In a combat situation, a pilot's need for the proper mind frame became magnified a hundredfold, for it often meant the difference between life and death.

There were three states of mind germane to a fighter pilot, two of which were deadly. The first deadly mindset was overconfidence. Even in 1945, this maxim rang true: "There are old pilots, and there are bold pilots. But there are no old, bold pilots." Jerry had learned that confidence in a pilot was the lifeline to survival, but overconfidence could quickly get one killed. He'd witnessed it before he left Hawaii, when his friends Bob Ferris and John Lindner lost their lives conducting overly aggressive dives while flying.

The other deadly mindset was lack of confidence. When a pilot got it into his head that he wasn't going to survive a mission, it was never a good thing. The issue occurred sometimes when a pilot panicked and became fearful, or when, because of fatigue or other factors, he lost his edge.

Jerry knew what that was like. On March 10, 1944, he'd experienced an engine lockup while piloting his P-40 over Hawaii. The plane's engine kicked into hyper-drive, and Jerry couldn't control it. He executed an emergency bailout and wound up spending nine hours in the Pacific before being rescued by a crash boat. The incident marked Jerry's closest brush with death before going into combat, and he'd been shaken up about it.

The next morning, however, Tapp came, got Jerry up, and put him back into the air. Tapp knew the only way to restore the young pilot's confidence was to get him flying again before doubt set in or his mind began playing tricks on him.

Now, Jerry worried that Phil was undergoing a similar dearth of confidence because of that weird premonition. Jerry's initial plan of getting Phil removed from today's mission had failed, so today, on the way to their pre-flight briefing, he tried snapping Phil out of his fatalistic mind frame instead. His hope was to restore Phil to the only safe mindset a pilot could have: calm confidence *before* the wheels of his plane left the runway.

"Whatever you do, just stay tight on my wing today, and you'll be okay," Jerry reassured him.

"Yes, captain."

"And remember, we've got Dumbos in the air all the way to Japan and all the way back, and they can pick [us] up out of the water if something goes wrong."

"Understand, captain."

"Plus we've got destroyers and subs all in the water if we need 'em. So just stay on my wing, and you'll be fine."

"Right, sir."

"We'll probably abort before we reach the target."

"Okay, Captain."

"Plus, if we hear the broadcast "UTAH," then the war's over, and we come home. Got it?"

"Got it, captain."

Jerry had tried.

But had anything he said worked?

■ ■ ■

The P-51s' mission that day started out well.

Cruising above the Pacific under the morning sun, the Americans had approached the Japanese coastline without incident. Jerry wondered how many more missions like this he would have to fly. They'd all thought the war was over, but now, here he was again, heading to strike a stubbornly resistant enemy.

But down below, in the nation they were about to attack, a philosophical battle was raging on whether to surrender or fight on. The "Big Six"—the six military officers running Japan—had been split by a vote of 3-3 on when and how to end the war with honor. In general, hard, passionate divisions of opinion existed among the Japanese military: some of the older officers wanted to surrender to prevent the destruction of Japan, while others wanted to fight on to the death and kill as many Americans as possible.

The previous night, while another three hundred American B-29s bombed Japan again, a group of rogue Japanese officers had started a coup against Prime Minister Suzuki and Emperor Hirohito. The officers burned the prime minister's office and surrounded the Imperial Palace, hoping to kidnap the emperor, all in an effort to prevent Japan's leadership from thinking about surrendering. For these officers, and for so many of the Japanese people, surrender was not an option. There was glory in death, but only shame in surrender; Japan, for its part, had never been invaded or lost a war in its history.

Fortunately for the rest of the world, the coup did not succeed. A group of senior Japanese officers talked the insurgents off the ledge, convincing them that there was nowhere to go. But while the revolt ended, the war did not, and so, with the shoreline of the enemy territory coming into view and Phil on his wing, Jerry knew it was time to go back to work.

On Jerry's order, all the planes in his squadron dropped their external fuel tanks over the ocean, then started their familiar aerial trek over the great, snow-capped peak of Mount Fuji. As of yet, there had been no radio signal with the word "UTAH."

As the Americans approached the Japanese capital, they began to identify targets. Within minutes, they swooped down over airfields and attacked despite heavy ground fire. Tracer bullets flew up from the Japanese guns as the Seventy-Eighth made multiple passes at each target. Phil stayed tight on Jerry's wing, just as instructed.

After strafing the last airfield, Jerry checked his fuel gauge and saw he was still in good shape. But when one of the pilots radioed that his tank had reached the ninety-gallon mark—the amount a Mustang needed for the return flight—it was time to pull up and begin plotting the course back to Iwo Jima.

Jerry looked over at Phil, who was still on his wing, and gave him a thumbs up.

Phil looked back and returned the gesture.

Confidence. Maybe it was working.

With the battle over Tokyo complete, Jerry set his course back out to the ocean and banked to the south. The three other Mustangs in Jerry's flight turned with him. A few moments later, as they approached the coast where they would rendezvous with the navigational B-29s, they neared a cloud cover in front of them, often the case when approaching the atmospheric temperature inversions near the coast. With Phil still tight on his wing, Jerry led the four Mustangs into the cloud bank. Flying at an altitude of about seven thousand feet, Jerry

First Lieutenant Phil Schlamberg, at age nineteen, was the final known combat death of World War II. *Photo Courtesy of Warren Hegg.*

focused his eyes on his navigation instruments, as the interior of the white, puffy clouds blocking his view of everything else.

But when the Mustangs emerged on the other side of the clouds, a devastating reality soon surfaced. Phil was gone. Most likely, he had been brought down by antiaircraft bullets fired into the clouds. There was no sign of him.

His premonition had come to pass.

Jerry was devastated.

When he landed at Iwo Jima, meanwhile, he learned something else: the war was over. The emperor had announced Japan's surrender three hours earlier, while Jerry and his flight were still over Japan. The code word "UTAH" had been broadcast to U.S. aircraft over the country, but the word had not reached the planes of the Seventy-Eighth until they landed.

It was a surreal feeling as Jerry climbed out of his plane and jumped down to the airfield, standing on a once-bloody Pacific island. Now, suddenly, it was a world at peace. The men of the Seventy-Eighth had a saying, "Alive in '45." That had been their goal, and now it was their reality. They were going home alive.

As Jerry walked away from his plane, another realization hit him: he had just flown the final combat mission of the war, and Phil Schlamberg, his dear friend, was the final combat death of the great war. One day, after Jerry had time to collect his emotions and his thoughts, the great historical significance of the mission he'd just flown would sink in. But for now, one thought consumed his mind:

At last, it was time to go home.

The Final Salute

Iwo Jima
March 31, 2015

Seventy years had passed since the end of World War II when Jerry Yellin stepped foot on Iwo Jima once again. It no longer looked like the war-zone that had greeted him as a twenty-one-year-old pilot. The winds of peace blowing gently across the Pacific proved much sweeter than the smell of death and war that had greeted him during his first stay on Iwo Jima. The mounds of dead bodies he'd witnessed on that first arrival were long since gone, and thousands of neatly maintained graves stood in silent tribute to the Marines who'd died to secure the island for the Allied war effort. The island itself had been turned back over to Japan, a nation that, within a generation, had gone from America's bitter enemy to trusted ally.

But the last living fighter pilot from that final mission over Japan had not come to celebrate all the changes that had occurred since 1945; he had returned at the invitation of the Japanese government to honor those with whom he had served. Here, on what had once been hell on earth, Japanese and American soldiers, sailors, airmen, and marines now stood together on a windswept day, saluting the handful of elderly warriors on both sides who were still alive. Jerry and a small number of American Iwo Jima veterans in their nineties stood side-by-side with, hugged, and even saluted a few of the equally old Japanese veterans who'd once been their mortal enemies. Many tears were shed for the fallen.

As for the men of Jerry's Seventy-Eighth Fighter Squadron, and the Seventh Fighter Command, most of them were gone now. Tapp, Vande Hey, and Crim had all became senior officers in the U.S. Air Force and lived to ripe old age before hearing the final call of Taps. Others, like White and Mathis, had given their golden years, a chance to raise a family and to die and rest in peace on the very soil of their homeland, to freedom's cause.

Jerry stood for both of them now, and for the three classmates who'd arrived together with him in Hawaii in 1943. Bob Roseberry had died on March 17, 2015, just two weeks before Jerry's return to Iwo Jima. Bob Ruby had eventually moved to Battle Creek, Michigan and died in November of 1999. Al Sherren, of course, had given his life to his country on July 8, 1945, over Tokyo.

Jerry stood, too, for Phil Schlamberg, whose death marked the end of the costliest war in human history. Phil's memory would be carried on not only by his fellow pilot, but by his niece, Melanie Sloan, who researched his legacy long after his death, and by his great-nieces, Vanessa and Scarlett Johansson, both well-known actresses. Even with the tremendous talent in his family, however, Phil—shot down and killed at the age of 19 in service to his country—was the family hero.

For as long as Jerry could stand on Iwo Jima, Phil and the rest of his fallen comrades would not be forgotten.

The veteran's face had worn over the passage of time. His body wasn't as strong as it had once been, nor was his coordination quite as sharp. But still, even seventy years later, he fit proudly into his khaki uniform, with his silver captain's bars pinned to his right collar. And his salute was as sharp as the day he had accepted his commission.

His own life had been a series of twists and turns, triumph and tears, hope and tragedy, patience and perseverance. He never married the girl named Doris for whom his plane had been named. But he had spent nearly a lifetime with the true love of his life, Helene, who he met on a blind date on Good Friday, 1949. Helene had passed away on June 23, 2015, after sixty-five wonderful years of marriage. Her loss, so late in life, would be the most painful of all for the old fighter pilot.

In perhaps the supreme irony of the veteran's life, meanwhile, his son would marry a Japanese girl and move to Japan, and Jerry would learn to love, respect, and commune with the very people that he had once, with all his might, tried to kill, and who had taken the lives of the fellow airmen closest to him.

Over the course of the war, Jerry had flown with a total of sixteen pilots who did not come back. And yet, there was no bitterness as his feet rested on the soil that had cost him and others so dearly.

"The greatest honor of my life," he declared before the ceremony started that wind-swept day on Iwo Jima, as he stood under the American flag brought to life by the powerful Pacific breeze, "was to serve my country."

Later, his aging hand would flash a final salute—a visible tribute to the invisible heroes now resting in peace in the heart of the island and depths of the sea.

He was the last fighter pilot of their heroic cause, and he would stand with them forever.

THE AIRMAN'S CREED

I am an American Airman.
I am a Warrior.
I have answered my Nation's call.
I am an American Airman.
My mission is to Fly, Fight, and Win.
I am faithful to a Proud Heritage,
A Tradition of Honor,
And a Legacy of Valor.
I am an American Airman.
Guardian of Freedom and Justice,
My Nation's Sword and Shield,
Its Sentry and Avenger.
I defend my Country with my Life.
I am an American Airman.
Wingman, Leader, Warrior.
I will never leave an Airman behind,
I will never falter,
And I will not fail.

General T. Michael Moseley
Chief of Staff
United States Air Force
April 27, 2007
Washington, D.C.

ACKNOWLEDGMENTS

"**N**o man is an island," the poet John Donne said nearly four hundred years ago. Likewise, this book isn't the product of an author isolated on an island, but rather of a team working together, each member with special roles, in sharp symmetry, to achieve the final result. To this team, my thanks are rendered below.

Special thanks to my "west coast editor," Jack Miller, of La Mesa, California, a veteran of the United States Army, a patron of the San Diego Zoo and the San Diego Wild Animal Park, and a supporter of the Lamb's Players Theatre in Coronado. Thanks also to my "east coast editor," Mary Lynne Landry, for her always-sharp editorial support.

A huge shout-out to the pros of the Regnery Publishing team, especially to editor Nancy Feuerborn and publicist Loren Long, two of the best in the business.

Thanks also to Alex Novak, Regnery's fine acquisitions editor, and to my dynamic literary agent Chip MacGregor. Both are visionaries who supported this book from the beginning.

Much appreciation goes to the Ronald Reagan Presidential Foundation for supporting *The Last Fighter Pilot* and for inviting us to launch the book at the Reagan Library in Simi Valley. As a junior in college, I attended President Reagan's first inauguration in 1981. Now, thirty-six years later, to have the Reagan Foundation's support of this book is a special personal honor.

The mother of two great actresses and a member of one of the nation's most talented families, Melanie Sloan is perhaps best known for her role in the entertainment industry. Now she leaves another great mark—this time as a historian. Melanie has diligently researched the life of her young uncle, First Lieutenant Phil Schlamberg, who on August 15, 1945, was killed in Japan, at the age of nineteen, becoming the final combat death of World War II. Thanks to Melanie for sharing her research, and for spending hours on the phone answering my questions. The nation owes her a debt of gratitude for introducing us to her heroic uncle, that he might finally take his rightful place in history.

Finally, there is Captain Jerry Yellin. The man is a national treasure, and my efforts to thank him fail at the outset, for it is impossible to fully acknowledge a patriot, or adequately describe a legend. I'm grateful that he let me try to tell part of his great story. As Jerry has said, "The greatest honor of my life was to serve my country." I'm blessed to call him a friend.

Don Brown
Charlotte, North Carolina
May 21, 2017

NOTES

CHAPTER 6

1. Allied war crimes tribunals later investigated this vicious and inhumane treatment of American flyers and prosecuted the Japanese officers after the surrender of Japan.

CHAPTER 13

1. Jerry's description is from an interview with the *New York Times* and is further recounted in his excellent biography, *Of War and Weddings*, Kindle edition (Friendswood: Total Recall Publishing, 2011), 321-323.
2. Ibid.

CHAPTER 16

1. The story is told by Jerry Yellin in *Of War and Weddings*, Kindle edition (Friendswood: Total Recall Publishing, 2011).

BIBLIOGRAPHY

MAJOR WORKS OF MILITARY NONFICTION

Bingham, Kenneth E. *Black Hell: The Story of the 133rd Navy Seabees On Iwo Jima February 19, 1945.* Charleston: CreateSpace Publishing, 2011.

Bush, George W. *41: A Portrait of My Father.* New York: Crown/Archetype, 2014.

Giangreco, D. M. *Hell to Pay: Operation Downfall and the Invasion of Japan, 1945–47.* Annapolis: Naval Institute Press, 2009.

Guillain, Robert. *I Saw Tokyo Burning: An Eyewitness Narrative from Hiroshima to Tokyo.* New York City: Doubleday, 1981.

Hammel, Eric. "The 78th on 7 April 1945." In *Aces at War: The American Aces Speak.* Pacifica: Pacifica Military History, 2007.

Hatch, Gardner N. and Frank H. Winter. *P-51 Mustang.* New York: Turner Publishing, 1993.

Lambert, John W. *Night of the Samurai: 26 March 1945 Banzai Attack on Airfield #2, (as told by Air Force Personnel who survived it).* In *The Pineapple Air Force: Pearl Harbor to Tokyo.* St. Paul: Phalanx Publishing, 1990.

Lambert, John W. "Black Friday on the Empire Run." In *The Long Campaign.* St. Paul: Phalanx Publishing, 2015.

O'Leary, Michael. *VIII Fighter Command at War.* London: Bloomsbury Publishing, 2012.

Tallentire, Karen Jo. *Fighting the Unbeatable Foe: Iwo Jima and Los Alamos.* Outskirts Press, 2015.

Werrell, Kenneth. *Blankets of Fire: US. Bombers over Japan During World War II.* Smithsonian Institute Publications, 1996).

Yellin, Captain Jerry. *Of War & Weddings: A Legacy of Two Fathers*. Friendswood: TotalRecall Publishing, 1995.

MILITARY AND AVIATION MAGAZINES

Pope, Stephen. "Constant Speed Prop Basics: Tips for Getting the Most out of Your Constant Speed Propeller," *Flying Magazine*, July 1, 2014.

Tillman, Barrett. "The Mustangs of Iwo Jima." *Airpower Magazine*, vol. 7, no. 1, pg. 30, January 1977.

Wolk, Herman S. "The Twentieth Against Japan," *Air Force Magazine*, April 2004.

NEWSPAPER SOURCES

Laurence, Charles. "George HW Bush Narrowly Escaped Comrades' Fate of Being Killed and Eaten by Japanese Captors," *The Telegraph* (London), February 6, 2017.

Niebuhr, Gustav. "Hiroshima; Enola Gay's Crew Recalls the Flight into a New Era," *The New York Times* (New York), August 6, 1995.

"Biography and Obituary of Brigadier General James Vande Hey," *Austin American-Statesman* on Jan. 6, 2010.

WEBSITE ARTICLES ATTRIBUTABLE TO SPECIFIC AUTHORS

Tapp, Major James B. "7th Fighter Command History," *7th Fighter Command Association*. Accessed March 1, 2017. http://www.7thfighter.com/history.html

Trueman, C. N. "The Fire Raids on Japan," *The History Learning Site*, www.historylearningsite.co.uk. May 19, 2015.

MILITARY GOVERNMENTAL SOURCES
AND PUBLICATIONS

OFFICE OF AIR FORCE HISTORY, Washington, DC, *Air Force Combat Units of World War II*, edited by Maurer Maurer (1983).

UNITED STATES AIR FORCE PUBLICATION, *47th Fighter Squadron AAF, A.P.O No. 86, HISTORY OF THE COMMAND SECTION (1-31 March 1945)* Document Declassified IAW Executive Order 12958.

UNITED STATES AIR FORCE PUBLICATION, *47th Fighter Squadron AAF, A.P.O No. 86, HISTORY OF THE COMMAND SECTION (1–30 April 1945)* Document Declassified IAW Executive Order 12958, signed April 17, 1995.

UNITED STATES AIR FORCE PUBLICATION, *47th Fighter Squadron AAF, A.P.O No. 86, HISTORY OF THE COMMAND SECTION (1–31 July 1945)* Document Declassified IAW Executive Order 12958, signed April 17, 1995.

OFFICIAL USAF BIOGRAPHY, "Biography of General Curtis Emerson LeMay," Accessed March 1, 2017, http://www.af.mil/About-Us/Biographies/Display/Article/106462/general-curtis-emerson-lemay/.

OFFICIAL USAF BIOGRAPHY, "Biography of Major General Ernest 'Mickey Moore," Accessed March 1, 2017, http://www.af.mil/About-Us/Biographies/Display/Article/106180/major-general-ernest-moore/.

OFFICIAL USAF BIOGRAPHY, "Biography of Major General Kenneth R. Powell," Accessed March 1, 2017, http://www.af.mil/About-Us/Biographies/Display/Article/105934/major-general-kenneth-r-powell/.

OFFICIAL USAF BIOGRAPHY, "Biography of Brigadier General James Vande Hey," http://www.af.mil/About-Us/Biographies/Display/Article/105310/brigadier-general-james-m-vande-hey/.

UNITED STATES ARMY AIR FORCE PUBLICATION. *P-51 Mustang Pilot's Flight Manual, AAF Manual 51-127-5*, USAAF and North American Aviation, Reprinted by Periscope Film, LLC (2006).

AMERICAN BATTLE MONUMENTS COMMISSION, Honolulu Memorial—Tablets of the Missing, "Identifying gravesite of 1st Lieutenant Philip Schlamberg, United States Army Air Forces," Accessed March 1, 2017, https://www.abmc.gov/database-search-results?search_api_aggregation_3=schlamberg&submit=Search.

MILITARY WEBSITE ARTICLES WITHOUT SPECIFIC AUTHOR ATTRIBUTION

"American Missions against Susaki Airfield (Chi Chi Jima Airfield) August 12, 1944–March 31, 1945," *Pacific Wrecks Website,* Accessed March 1, 2017, http://www.pacificwrecks.com/airfields/japan/susaki/index.html/.

"Awards and Citations to Major James Buckley Tapp—Distinguished Flying Cross Citation for Extraordinary Heroism on 7 April 1945," *Military Times—Hall of Valor,* Accessed March 1, 2017, http://valor.militarytimes.com/recipient.php?recipientid=22979.

"Before the 506th Arrived—7 April 1945—First VLR Mission to Japan"—History of the 506th Fighter Group," *506th Fighter Group Official Website,* Accessed March 1, 2017, www.506thfightergroup.org.

"Composite list of P-51 Mustang Aces of WWII," *Mustangs.com Website,* Accessed March 1, 2017," http://www.mustangsmustangs.com/p-51/aces/aces_list.

"Fighting Ends on Iwo Jima—March 16, 1945," *This Day in History,* Accessed March 1, 2017, http://www.history.com/this-day-in-history/fighting-on-iwo-jima-ends.

"North American P-51 Pilot's Check List," *Aerofiles,* Accessed March 1, 2017, http://www.aerofiles.com/checklist-p51.html.

"The Incendiary Bombing Raids on Tokyo, 1945," *EyeWitness to History,* www.eyewitnesstohistory.com (2004).

"The 78th Fighter Squadron, the 'Bushmasters' of the 'Pineapple Air Force,'" *Hawaii Aviation Preservation Society,* Accessed March 1, 2017, http://hiavps.com/78th%20FS.htm.

"Unit History 506th Fighter Group, (Including 457th, 458th and 462nd Fighter Squadrons) 1–30 June 1945," *7th Fighter Command Association,* Accessed March 1, 2017, http://www.7thfighter. com/506thfg/history/506th_history_june_1945.pdf.

CHAPTER ONE

The Journey

I saw Japan for the first time from the cockpit of a P-51 on April 7, 1945. We were the first land-based fighter planes to fly a mission against the Japanese Empire. At the morning briefing before take off, the intelligence officer told us, "When you fly across Suruga Bay, focus your gun cameras on the tip of Mount Fuji. In that way we will be able to evaluate your film when you fire your guns at the enemy." We needed a centering point for the rings of our gun sight, to see if our guns were firing where they were aimed. The mountain loomed skyward to twelve thousand feet, its snow-covered peak glistened in the morning sun, a picture indelibly imprinted on my mind.

In October 1982 my wife, Helene, and I boarded a Singapore Airline 747 at Los Angeles International Airport for a flight to Tokyo. It had been thirty-seven years since I had flown the last mission against my World War II enemy. I had received an invitation to go to Japan for three weeks on a business trip as part of a lecture team. It was the first time that I had thought about Japan as a place to visit. I hadn't dwelt on the war, or even thought much about it, until then.

It was over, and I had lived my life without looking back. Never had I spoken of my war experiences. Occasionally I mentioned flying, or bailing out off the coast of Hawaii to my children. But I had never gone into any detail about my life as a combat pilot, not even to Helene. As I settled back in the comfortable business-class seat, my mind drifted back in time.

On my eighteenth birthday, February 15, 1942, I had enlisted in the Army Air Corps. The application required my parents' signatures before I could take the examination for Aviation Cadet. They held back as long as they could. They were not eager for me to go off to war and thought I should wait to be drafted.

Reluctantly, my parents signed the necessary papers. I passed the mental exam but failed the physical when it was discovered that I had only 20/30 vision in the left eye. The doctor said I could take the test again in a week and would be accepted into the program if I passed then. I remained in a darkened room and ate carrots for three days prior to the examination. As luck would have it, my mother was on the draft board and she brought me the eye chart to memorize! I passed the test the second time and in August 1942 I reported for induction into the Army Air Corps as an Aviation Cadet.

My obsession was to fly a fighter plane against the Japanese....

Images of war were engraved in the minds of all of us who had been in combat. They surfaced from time to time, day or night, triggered by events, something we heard, or they just crept into our minds at odd times. It happened to me once in a movie theater. Helene and I had flown to San Francisco to celebrate our son Michael's thirtieth birthday. Michael was a resident physician at Pacific Presbyterian Medical Center. The day after the party was miserable and cold, so we all decided to see a film. The movie *Platoon* had just opened and had received good reviews. Helene suggested that we see it. Michael; his wife, Gail; David, our oldest son; Helene; and I went to the film together. I was not prepared for what I saw on the screen nor for what happened to me.

The movie was a devastating story of ground soldiers in Vietnam, their fight to survive the war and their inner, tormented battles to maintain some sense of humanity. I drifted off from time to time, inward to my memory, a memory of war that I had carried for forty-one years. As the screen showed bodies being thrown into a large pit, a bulldozer moving dirt and dead bodies into a mass grave, I started to cry uncontrollably.

When the film ended I couldn't get out of my seat. I sat there and sobbed for fifteen minutes. Helene looked alarmed and kept stroking my head. When I calmed down, Michael asked, "What happened, Dad? Are you all right?"

"I'll be all right in a minute. It's just...the screen showed pictures that have been in my mind all these years...Japanese soldiers, mounds of them, slowly being pushed into mass graves on Iwo Jima."

As soon as I was able, we left the theater and walked the rainy streets of San Francisco for an hour. Helene never let go of my hand. That night I spoke to her about the war for the first time.

In the spring of 1945, I flew my P-51 from Saipan to Iwo Jima to join the war against the Japanese. The Marines had landed on Iwo in February and secured a dirt runway at the foot of Mount Suribachi, memorialized by the famous photograph of Marines raising the flag on its summit. I was a member of the Seventy-Eighth Fighter Squadron assigned to the Seventh Fighter Wing, under the command of Brigadier General Mickey Moore. I landed on that dirt runway.

We dive-bombed and strafed the Japanese defenders who were dug deeply into caves in the hillsides of the island. The Marine mortuary was alongside our squadron base and every day we saw truckloads of U.S. Marines, killed in battle, being brought in and laid out for identification and burial. Everywhere we looked there were hills of bulldozed Japanese bodies, and the smell of death filled the air. Later, mass graves were dug and the bodies were pushed into the ground and covered.

We lived in foxholes dug into the sand and rock of the island. On the ground, we fought to survive terrifying Banzai raids, which were suicide attacks by *sake*-drunk Japanese defenders who thought it an honor to die, so long as they took as many enemy soldiers as possible with them. From the air, we dropped napalm into cave openings, driving the Japanese soldiers out to waiting Marine rifle and mortar fire.

We went to the front, looking for souvenirs in the same caves we had dive-bombed and strafed. There we saw the results of flame-throwers, "freezing" soldiers into hideous positions. And we attended memorial services for our fellow pilots, for whom the war had ended. What I saw on Iwo has remained with me ever since.

Now, as the 747 approached Japan after the long flight over the Pacific from California, I asked the steward to see if he could get me into the cockpit. This is forbidden on domestic airlines but permissible on some foreign carriers at the discretion of the captain.

"Please tell him an old World War II fighter pilot wants to see Japan again from a pilot's perspective, to view Mount Fuji as he saw it on his first day in combat."

A few minutes later the steward returned with a message:

"The captain asks that you come up to the flight deck whenever you desire, Mr. Yellin. He will be delighted to have you."

I left my seat immediately and entered the huge cockpit of this giant airliner. After introducing me to the co-pilot and the engineer, the captain extended an invitation to stay for the landing. I gladly accepted. Then, as I sat down on the jump seat behind the pilot, I looked out of the cockpit window in the direction of Fuji. I caught sight of the famous peak but my mind froze on another image—I saw again the faces of my dead comrades, the piles of Marine bodies waiting identification, the bloated, maggot-filled bodies of the Japanese soldiers. The smell of death filled my nostrils once more.

Overcome with emotion, I had to leave the cockpit and compose myself, before we landed in Tokyo.

The first few days in Japan were extremely difficult. I did not tell Helene, though she must have suspected. As we walked through the streets of Tokyo, I would catch her looking at me as I stared up at the sky. I saw the lights of a thousand bombs exploding across the ground. I saw crippled, burning planes falling from the sky. I pictured the B-29s dropping their bombs on the city.

The sights were triggering more memories than I was prepared for. They came into my awareness as I looked into the faces of the people on the streets and, disturbingly, as I lay in bed at night. I needed some quieter space to let my mind recuperate from the sudden, unexpected onslaught.

CHAPTER TWO

Sen

It has always been easy for me to talk to strangers when we travel and, sometimes, to make friends. In England one year, we needed directions to a subway. When I asked my seat mate at a concert where the nearest entrance was, he not only described where it was but walked with us to make sure we found it. The next day he called our hotel and invited us for lunch. We became friends. I didn't expect that in Japan for several reasons, the least of which was the language barrier and my unresolved feelings about the war. I was wrong.

We met Sen Matsuda quite by accident on the bullet train (Shinkansen) that travels the Tokaido Line from Tokyo to Osaka. He was seated with his wife in the first car. I noticed him immediately as we scanned the car for an empty seat.

He looked like a Buddha. His smooth, brown skin was taut on the bones of his face, and he had large beautiful eyes. He was clearly an elderly man, quite gaunt, but without wrinkles. He was elegantly dressed in blue leather pants and a brown leather jacket. His eyes sparkled and shone.

He was looking my way as I placed the luggage on the rack over the seats. Our eyes met for an instant and I knew that I would have to speak with him before we reached our destination.

He too felt something pass between us in that short contact of our eyes. He told me that later as we talked.

Soon after we pulled out of the station, vendors moved through the cars selling hot tea and coffee. These were followed by girls selling box lunches. Most of our fellow travelers bought something, and soon they were busy eating. The boxes were made of wood and were wrapped and tied with string or ribbon. At each station, as passengers left, they placed their re-tied boxes neatly in a pile. The boxes were collected at several stops. Absolutely no litter was left by anyone.

The opportunity to meet Mr. Matsuda came when I had a problem purchasing a cup of tea from the vendor. Noticing my difficulty expressing my wishes to her in Japanese, he leaned across the aisle and softly whispered, in perfect English, "She doesn't sell tea, only coffee."

"*Arigato Gozimasu*," I said, and he responded again in perfect English, "Don't mention it." With that, our friendship began.

Spontaneously, we both got up and, standing in the aisle of the rapidly moving train, introduced our selves.

"Your face glows with energy and contentment," I said, "and I felt I had to speak with you."

We exchanged business cards and started talking about the book he was holding.

"It's an Australian novel," he said. "I'm reviewing it for a friend." He paused. I had never heard of the book. "By the way," he asked, "have you read the book *Roots* by Alex Haley?"

"Of course," I replied. "It is one of my favorites. I bought copies of it for several of my friends just after it was published."

He looked at me for a moment and said, "I translated it into Japanese." He did not say this to impress me (although it certainly did), but to convey the fact that he knew a lot about America.

The train was approaching our stop, and I was afraid that we would not see each other again. Just before we started to gather our luggage together, he asked if we would be able to visit him in Chigasaki City before we left Japan.

"Please come to our home for lunch," he said. "We can continue our talk then."

"We have a tight schedule. I'll have to call you. I hope we can arrange it."

We shook hands warmly, the train stopped, and from the platform, we waved good-bye to our new friend.

I wanted to spend some time with Sen Matsuda, our new friend from the train. I had our schedule rearranged to include lunch with Mr. Matsuda the day before our trip to Kyoto.

The ride to his home in Chigasaki City, a suburb of Tokyo, took an hour. As our train eased to a stop at the station, we saw him standing on the platform, peering into each car as it passed, looking for us. He was dressed in a beautiful, full-length kimono. As we stepped off the train, he walked slowly toward us, accompanied by a young lady.

His daughter, Midori, had arrived from Tokyo a few minutes earlier, summoned to help her mother with the lunch. Midori looked much like her father. She had a warm, friendly face and a personality to match. The four of us walked out of the station for the short taxi drive to their home.

When we arrived at the house, we were greeted by Mrs. Matsuda. She was smaller than Sen, about five foot two, quite thin and slight, and spoke English well. She greeted us with warmth and gestured for us to follow. Much to our surprise, instead of the sparsely furnished Japanese decor that we had expected, we saw a room completely furnished in a Western mode. We sat on a large stuffed Victorian-style couch in front of a low antique coffee table. Mr. and Mrs. Matsuda each sat on high-backed stuffed chairs on either side. The floor was covered with a Persian carpet.

Mrs. Matsuda served us tea and sweets, according to the custom. My friend thanked us for coming. "I am honored," he said. "I did not think that I could make new friends, especially foreign ones, at my age. I am seventy-five now, and nearing the end of my life."

"Come now," I replied. "You look fit and have a healthy inner glow."

"Yes, that is true, but I have had surgery for cancer, and you know what that can mean. I am aware that I can pass on at any time, so I have been spending all of these precious days in beautiful places, and looking at beautiful things. I want to live the rest of my life seeing and hearing only the wonders that man has created. I want to remember only the beauty. I want to view again all of the natural wonders of my country, so that I can take them with me when I begin the next great journey."

Mrs. Matsuda and Midori prepared lunch in the kitchen while Helene and I sat talking to Sen, sipping a fine Bordeaux. When Mrs. Matsuda called us to the dining room, a huge pot that smelled delicious was steaming on the table.

"I must flavor our lunch," he said. "This is a recipe for *sukiyaki* that my father taught me, and it has to be just so. My wife doesn't trust her taste and wants me to finish flavoring the dish." We watched as he poured *sake* from a large bottle, then, smelling the steam, he added other ingredients.

When he was satisfied, we were asked to join the family for lunch. We ate on dishes using Western utensils.

Lunch was exquisite. We ate and talked for more than an hour. At times I felt I was with old, dear friends. But I also thought, "This man had been my enemy." He was the first Japanese man I had met who spoke English well enough and was of the age that he might have served in the military. I gathered my courage and asked him about his experiences in the war.

When he replied, he spoke slowly and carefully. "I was a young man when my country began its preparation for war," he said. "I was born in 1914, the year that World War I started, and I spent my early years in Tokyo. When I was seventeen, Japan began its disastrous adventure by invading Manchuria. Our people were told that we needed to become completely self-sufficient: no dependency on the outside world for the raw materials necessary to sustain our needs. The oil and minerals in China would help Japan become a 'self-sufficient' nation.

"Of course, we were never told about the atrocities committed by our invading armies, or our brutal treatment of the Chinese people. All that we saw or heard were glowing stories of the conquest and the brightness of Japan's future.

"I only learned about our history when I went to the United States to study in 1938. Your newspapers and newsreel movies showed pictures that I could not, did not, want to believe. I clearly remember a photograph of a small baby crying in the streets while fires burned around her in the bombed city.

"I have never, ever forgotten that picture. It remained with me when I returned home to Japan in 1940.

"The plans to fight a war with the United States and the Soviet Union had already become apparent in 1936 when a change in our government gave power to supporters of our aggressive military command. Not satisfied with the success in China, they formulated a five-year plan, agreed to by the Diet, to build a 'fighting-machine' large enough to take on the United States and the Soviet Union. Our leaders felt that victories over these two countries would secure Japan's position as the dominant force in Asia.

"The plan was truly audacious. It called for the build-up of war materials from the country we would use them on, the United States. Japan's steel production would be tripled with the purchase of iron and oil from America. Factories would be built with machines from the United States and Germany. A stockpile of raw materials would be accumulated for sustaining an all-out war for two years, the time our leaders thought it would take to win.

"None of this was revealed to the public. I only became aware of the depth of planning after I graduated from college and joined the government as an economist.

"I was opposed to the war from the beginning. My father and I both attended school in America. Not only did we not believe what we were being told by our government, we knew the might of your country firsthand. The newspapers were full of speeches by our military leaders. 'The Americans have no stomach for war,' they said. 'All they are interested in is having good times. When we start the war, they will last for two weeks, surrender, and then we can proceed to occupy the territories we want and need for our expanding economy.'

"We knew better but were desperately afraid to speak up. I worked for the government, and I know that my views were shared by many. I truly felt the Emperor could have prevented the war, but he did nothing except echo the words of the military leaders.

"Then came what our government called 'the glorious attack on Pearl Harbor.'"

Matsuda Sen drifted off into silence and we sat for a long time caught up in our private memories.

Suddenly I heard Mr. Matsuda's voice again. I had missed some of his words, but I forced myself to tune back in.

"I was determined to live through the war," he was saying. "I knew that we would be attacked in due time, and I prepared myself for that eventuality. We were all issued helmets and gas masks. Every day there were drills on what to do if Tokyo was attacked. I listened and learned well. I never left my helmet anywhere. It was with me wherever I went, and this was years before any serious aerial bombing began. My colleagues made jokes, sometimes to my face, but I did not care. I was not going to die in a war from lack of protection. If my time came, so be it, but I would not be left unprotected.

"When the B-29s finally came they were terrifying. The fire bombs would outline an area and then uncountable bombs were dropped inside the fires. The explosions were devastating. The fires ran unchecked throughout the city.

"One day my assistant left the office for home only to return in a complete daze. He could not find a trace of his house, and his entire family was missing. Wife, children, mother, father; all gone. He had no one to turn to, no place to live. For weeks he wandered through our office building as if in a dream. He slept in the office, ate in the office, and finally came to accept his fate. All of us suffered losses. No one escaped some tragedy. And still I carried my helmet. It became my shield against danger, even after the 'all clear' had sounded.

"Once the bombings started, Tokyo became the most dangerous place in the Empire, even more dangerous than the front. And still our leaders thought we would defeat America, but they had awakened a sleeping giant that would not rest until we were conquered.

"I remember one raid in particular. It was in April and began in midmorning. The bombers were escorted by American fighters for the first time. They came in much lower than before and we could see wave after wave filling the entire sky for hours. Again the fires started and then the winds began to blow. The fire spread from section to section and by evening were lighting the night sky like daylight. I lived many miles from the fires, but at eleven that night I could read a newspaper in the street in front of my house. That's how light it was. On that day eighty thousand Japanese died, and that was only the beginning."

CHAPTER THREE

The War

I watched Mr. Matsuda intently as he calmly recounted his story. Tears slowly welled up in my eyes as I listened to his words.

I had flown on that first escorted raid.

I remember telling a war correspondent from the *New York Times* that I saw little dots of light spring from the ground as the bombs exploded. Wave after wave of bombers dropped their cargo inside the squares of fire on the ground. We fighter pilots were in a constant state of alert; Japanese fighters were all over the sky and the aerial battles between us were fierce. We had to protect our "Big Brothers"—the B-29s—as they droned on and on over the target. When I had a chance to look down, I could see fires raging. All of the city, it seemed, was on fire.

Triggered by Mr. Matsuda's words, memories started to come back in a flood.

His words recreated images in my mind that I had tried desperately to forget. At that moment the past was as real as the present—I had slipped back in time. It was shortly after we had set up base on lwo Jima. We knew we had been shipped to lwo to fly combat missions, but suddenly we had our first order.

The sixteen senior pilots in our squadron were to fly eight hundred miles over the waters of the Pacific to Japan, in single-engine fighter planes, to escort B-29s of the Seventy-Third Bomber Wing as they attacked the Nakajima aircraft plant at Tokyo. We would protect the bombers from Japanese fighter planes until their work was done; then we would turn around and fly the eight hundred miles back to Iwo Jima.

This was to be the first "Very Long Range Fighter Escort" of B-29s over Japan. Only pilots with eight hundred to one thousand hours of flying were chosen. There would be well over four hundred B-29s, and a total of one hundred fighter pilots flying P-51 Mustangs. Takeoff was at 7:00 a.m. We were to be over the target from 10:45 a.m. till 11:30 a.m., and expected to return to Iwo again at 2:15 in the afternoon.

We took off and assembled in formation. Major John Piper of the Forty-Seventh Squadron was the group leader. Gil Snipes led the Forty-Fifth and Jim Vande Hey led the Seventy-Eighth—my squadron.

We rendezvoused with the B-29s at 18,000 feet over Kozu Shima, an island off the coast of the Izu Peninsula. Each fighter was carrying a heavy load, with two 110-gallon drop-tanks. As we crossed the coast of the mainland, we dropped the wing tanks and prepared to face enemy aircraft. The P-5ls of the Seventy-Eighth Fighter Squadron were flying the right front quarter position, leading the whole formation and thus becoming the first land-based fighter squadron over mainland Japan.

Everything seemed to be going smoothly. We had climbed to thirty thousand feet to be "high cover," protecting the bombers from attack. It was from there that I watched the bombs explode like tiny firecrackers in the city. I could see pinpoints of light where the bombs hit, and then the sparks would come together to form a massive fire with thick black smoke that rose to twenty-five thousand feet.

The fighting and the flak was intense. At one point I saw one of our B-29s get hit, and the right wing fell off. The plane burst into flames, and then, as if it were all being photographed in slow motion, one parachute came out, then a second, and a third; then the huge, lumbering plane just keeled over like a ship in the water, went into a spin, and fell from the sky. Of the twelve crew members on board, only three had bailed out.

We stayed over Japan for nearly an hour; then, when one of our pilots called in that he was running low on fuel, we turned for home. By 2:30 p.m., all of the aircraft had landed back at Iwo.

Despite seven hours and thirty-five minutes of exhausting over-water flying and nearly an hour of life-and-death combat with Japanese aircraft, every single fighter pilot got back safely. Of the bombers, only three were lost; two by anti-aircraft fire and only one, possibly, brought down by enemy aircraft. A total of eighty Japanese planes were destroyed.

Upon landing we found how dangerously low on fuel we were. I had only eight gallons left in my tank. What we didn't know then, was that we had run into what would later be called the "jet stream"—200 mph winds that we flew into head-on all the way back from Japan. That's why we nearly ran out of gas.

Most of us had difficulty just getting out of our planes. We had been sitting in those tight cockpits for almost eight hours, flying without automatic pilots, navigating without navigation equipment. I was helped out of the plane by my crew chief. Hardly able to stand, we walked to a tent for the debriefing of that historic mission. Some one said his "butt was sprung," so that became the name for the condition; butt sprung.

A few weeks later a large Quonset hut was erected and equipped with bathtubs made of 100-gallon wing tanks that had been cut in half. Massage tables lined the entire side of the room. The tubs were filled with steaming hot, smelly, sulfur water just before we returned from a mission. From then on, we were debriefed and then taken to the "Olde Iwo Jima Spa" for a hot bath, cold beer, and a sandwich. Iwo means sulfur in Japanese. The water came out of the underground hot springs at 130°F. The Navy construction battalion, fondly known as the Seabees, tapped into the underground water supply, connected hoses and a pump, and the spa was born. Their reward was a substantial supply of hard liquor, courtesy of the flight surgeons office. After the hot bath and massage, our first priority was sleep. For me, that was hard to come by.

I remember telling the flight surgeon about the tremendous letdown after we began the flight home. I had watched my gas gauge go steadily down to empty, knowing I had to switch tanks or my engine would quit, yet not caring. Other pilots described similar experiences.

On the next and all subsequent missions, we were given benzedrine to take, one hour before we reached our target area. We'd fly two hours, take a pill, go on to the target, do our work, then fly four hours home. An hour after our interrogation, I would fall flat on my face with exhaustion as the drug wore off. All of us lost weight. I started the war weighing 160 pounds, but I weighed only 126 pounds at the end.

Our routine was to fly one long-range mission, followed by a local mission on Iwo and a short-range mission to knock out radar on nearby Chichi Jima. Then we would begin the rotation over by flying a long-range mission again, to the Japanese mainland. I flew each mission three times—once the night before, then the actual mission itself, and then again in vivid detail after I returned.

The evening before a mission, our names would be posted on the board. We knew we would be flying the next day, but we didn't know what the mission was, where the targets were, whether we would escort bombers or carry rockets—we just knew we had an assignment. For me, those nights were always sleepless, full of speculations and visions of possible destinations, with all their potential dangers.

We generally received information about the mission at a briefing before sunrise and then took off for Japan. As soon as we returned, practically as soon as we hit the runway, the questions began. Our crew chief would grab us first. He wanted to know if the airplane had performed properly. "Did everything work okay? Did you get in to the target?" Sometimes engines ran rough or guns wouldn't fire and the pilot would abort his mission, remaining with the escort B-29 off the coast of Japan. This was a concern for the crew chief, and they always asked how the engine performed. They took great pride in their work and did not like to let their pilot down.

Then while in the hot bath and with a cold beer, we were interrogated by the intelligence officers.

"What did you see?"

"What did you do?"

"Any kills?"

"What was the flak like?"

"How was the weather?"

"Were the maps accurate?"

We were in an agitated emotional state. They shot questions at us like reporters at a press conference and expected complete, detailed answers.

We answered as well as we could. The images in our minds at the time were extremely vivid, but we were so charged up that it was hard to talk.

After the debriefing, there was another round of questioning. All the other men involved in the airplanes—the armorers, the mechanics, the weather officers—had been waiting on the ground for seven or eight hours while we were away. They were a vital part of the team, but they saw nothing that happened, and they wanted to know!

And of course there were the other pilots. We were all feeling very emotional, whooping it up, in a tremendous state of excitation. It was partly the drug we were given—the benzedrine—but it was also because of what we had just gone through, and because we were back. We had made it.

We went around to each other, all talking at once, questioning one another, telling stories of what was seen or done.

Then the benzedrine wore off, and the beer wore off, and we went to bed exhausted. But I couldn't sleep, because the images were still going through my head. So I flew the mission again—re-living what I'd seen and done and reflecting on all the things that could have gone wrong. And if anybody was killed or missing, if one of us didn't come back, there was that to think about too....

Suddenly I realized that the room was silent. Mr. Matsuda was looking at me, quietly and patiently, with no irritation. I did not know how long I had been lost in memories. He continued his story.

"On the day the war ended, I stripped the blackout curtains from my windows and, looking toward the heavens, I shouted, 'I have lived! I have lived!' I was grateful for my life and for the lives of my family.

"Our soldiers came home from the war to a country that was nearly destroyed. Almost every city had suffered unimaginable damage. For the first time in my memory, I could see Mount Fuji from Tokyo, nearly sixty miles away. No buildings stood to block the view. The population was homeless, without food—and without spirit. The glory of war had turned to the reality of horrendous defeat, humiliation, and death. Our children, our women, our elders could be seen scratching through the rubble for food and clothing. There was no electricity and hardly any fuel to cook what little rice was available.

"It was September when the first contingent of American soldiers arrived in Japan. No one knew how they would behave.

"It must have been a strange sight for your soldiers in the early days of the occupation. Only our oldest men dared venture into the streets. Our women and children were kept inside and at times hidden from sight, their sounds muffled for fear of being detected. For years the Japanese people had been told of the barbarous Americans: how they ate young children, raped and killed all women and terrorized the population! Our soldiers were told that if they became prisoners, their arms would be hacked off and the bones made into letter openers that would be sold in America.

"We always were told of their cruelty. We knew from our own long history, and the history of other nations, that the defeated would be subjected to severe punishment and treatment. This was the way of the conqueror. We were totally unprepared for the attitude of your occupation forces. They were not anything like we thought they would be. The soldiers were so tall, so well fed. And they were gentle. Our children were given food and candy almost from the first day of the occupation. Soup kitchens were set up and, gradually, all of our people were given food. It was the beginning of a new way of life for all of us, and it was made easier by the kindness of the American troops.

"The signing of the surrender treaty in Yokohama Bay was a day that signaled a complete change in the Japanese way of life. Shortly after the signing, Emperor Hirohito spoke on the radio for the very first time. All of Japan fell to its knees as he outlined what was expected of us. No matter what was asked by the occupying forces, we were to do it. We were to obey them as if it were he himself talking. Japan must be obedient to the laws established by the Americans.

"'Our way of life will change,' he told us. 'All must accept this new life, as if I myself have ordained it. We must maintain our dignity and work hard to rebuild our cities, our country, our place in the world. I can assure you that we will be treated fairly by the American military forces. They have assured me that they will not interfere with our internal way of life.'"

Quietly I said, "Matsuda San, I was on that first fighter mission over Tokyo. I watched from the sky what you experienced on the ground."

Mr. Matsuda looked at me then closed his eyes. I fell silent, withdrew into myself. We sat in this tomb of silence for quite some time, thinking about what we had been talking about, what was happening in the room. I remember putting my hands over my eyes, and in the darkness, my thoughts turned to my childhood.

My sister and I often used to bring home stray kittens, lost dogs, and wounded birds. My mother helped us feed them milk using eye-droppers. From her and the animals, we learned about life, how precious it was. We tried to be as gentle with our charges as their mothers might. I thought about the Boy Scouts and remembered the Scout Oath. It began, "On my honor I will do my duty to God and my country, to obey the scout law." A scout is reverent, helpful, and the rest. The scouts taught me about nature, how to live in the woods, always to protect the environment, never to leave a fire without making sure it was out. And then I thought about April 7, 1945. How I had flown my P-51 over the home we were sitting in now, protecting the B-29s as they dropped their lethal loads, watching gleefully as the bombs exploded and the fires spread, thinking that the people below me were just "Japs"—my enemies.

It never occurred to me that a man like Sen might be on the ground hearing and feeling the bombs explode around him. He must have heard the cries of pain from the maimed, the cries of anguish from the injured and dying. It must have been terrible to live like that, day after day, unable to do anything but sit and wait for the bombers to return. How was it possible that my values had been altered so quickly, that I could enjoy a war as much as I did, that I could help kill thousands of people because my country said I should? I disliked myself intently at that moment. After what must have been only a few minutes, I opened my eyes and looked at my new friend, Sen Matsuda.

I thought, "Here I am in a foreign land, sitting with a man I have met only once, talking about the most profound experience of my life." We belonged to two cultures, two countries, which had been bitter enemies in our lifetimes. And now, in a suburb of Tokyo, we were talking about the past, about that war, the killing, feeling toward one another as old and loving friends. It was a moving experience.

Time was running out on our visit. Mr. Matsuda excused himself for a few minutes and returned dressed in a splendid brown suit with a dark shirt and light tie. We said our good-byes to Midori and Mrs. Matsuda, and walked to the taxi she had called. As we walked to the waiting cab, Sen donned a hat, took his walking stick in hand and joined us for the ride to the station. We were to spend a few more minutes together on the train. He was going to Hakone to attend his high school class reunion. As the train pulled into the Atami station, he stood up slowly and took my hand in his.

"I am sorry that we met so late in your trip, and so late in my life," he said. "But I am grateful that we have had even this little time to spend together. Please come back again soon."

The train stopped, he stepped off, turned, and stood waving as our train pulled out of the station.

Helene took my hand as we walked back to our seats. I was staring out of the window trying to cope with what we had heard, when Helene said, "I'm having a hard time keeping from crying."

"Me, too. I wonder why we met this man at this time and spent a day with him? I really wanted to hear about the war from a man his age. I just never expected anything like this to happen on this trip. I wonder how many more Sens live here; lived here when I was flying over their country?"

That night I couldn't sleep. I was upset by the memories that had begun surfacing as Mr. Matsuda told about his experiences during the war. And the feelings—anger, hatred, fear! I remembered what I had felt about the Japanese. The rage within me at the time was genuine. Some of what I felt came from what my mother told me when I began dating.

"How would you feel if you found a man had entered our home and was molesting your sister?" she asked me.

"I would kill him," I replied.

"Well, just remember that the girl you are dating tonight might have a brother who feels the same about his sister as you feel about yours."

That is how I felt about the Japanese. They had invaded my home, my country, and I would have to make them pay. All of the stories we began to hear from Corrigidor and Bataan, the indignation fueled by American propaganda that depicted the Japanese as "monsters," all contributed to my hatred for an entire nation of people. Now I had to look at them, and at me, from a different perspective.

I got up from the bed and went outside for a walk. It seemed so bizarre. At the same time that I was having these horrible memories about war, I was here walking the streets of Tokyo, late at night, a foreigner, one of the only Caucasians on the streets, and I felt perfectly safe, more safe and comfortable, in fact, than I would feel in my own country. And these were the streets that we had bombed nearly forty years ago!

I thought of the fear that our attacks must have caused in the people. And now, I felt no fear. The people were truly warm, helpful, and unthreatening. Whenever we needed help during our travels, we were directed to our destination by attentive strangers who made us feel welcome. We were always treated politely and courteously.

It was strange, I thought, that I felt no anger towards the Japanese people. But I was angry and I didn't know why. "It is appalling," I thought. "We keep repeating the same scenario over and over again only in different places with different people." I walked for hours before I returned to my hotel, feeling somewhat better, resolving nothing, my anger abated.

Helene had been worried by my absence. When I returned she asked me what was wrong.

"Nothing. I just couldn't sleep."

She knew that there was much more but did not press me further. She sensed my discomfort and anger, but she respected my silence. The next day we went to Kyoto.

CHAPTER FOUR

Discovering Japan

Helene and I were anxiously looking forward to seeing the gardens and temple buildings of Kyoto that we had seen only in pictures. Our guidebook listed all of the shrines in the area as well as the best time to view them. It was autumn and the leaves were beginning to change. We left the hotel, had the doorman call a taxi, and I told the driver "*Arashiyama*." I repeated it two or three times before the doorman leaned into the cab and said "*Arashiyama*."

"*Ah so, Arashiyama*," the driver repeated and pulled away.

Helene looked at me and laughed, "I thought you learned the language."

I had studied Japanese for four months before we left San Diego. "I thought so, too," I replied. "Didn't I say the same thing they said?"

We drove along a fast-flowing river for thirty minutes, then across a bridge where the driver stopped his taxi and said "*Arashiyama*."

According to the guidebooks, this is one of the most beautiful areas of Kyoto—both in the spring at cherry blossom time and in the fall for the brilliant display of nature's many colors. We were not disappointed. We walked along the lake, viewing the gardens, feeling the solitude one feels with nature; in spite of the fact that it seemed every schoolchild in Japan was also out there, surrounding us! The approach to the gardens was blocked by photographers lining up high school students to take their class pictures.

As noon approached we began to look for a restaurant to eat lunch. All were crowded with students. In one we spotted two empty seats next to two girls, aged about eighteen, and the host asked if we would sit next to them. They both smiled shyly, hiding their smiles behind their hands so we would not see their teeth.

I said "*Konichiwa*." ("Good afternoon.")

They said "Hello" (which came out "Herro"!), and we all laughed. Their lunch ended sooner than ours and they left, smiling and waving over their shoulders as they looked back at us.

Helene and I finished our *udon* (noodles) soon after, paid the check and left the restaurant to continue sightseeing. Neither of us expected to see our two table-mates again. However, they were standing a few feet from the entrance door, obviously waiting for us to appear. They bowed slightly as we approached them, and one girl said, "My name is Takako, and this is my friend Hisako. We are students in Hatoyama High School. We are on a school trip. We visited Nara, Hiroshima, and now, Kyoto."

"Yes," joined in Hisako, shyly. "Our teacher has asked us to speak to foreigners we meet and ask them a few questions. May we ask you our questions?"

"Of course," I replied.

They handed each of us a sheet of paper that read, "Our school class is studying peace. We have just returned from Hiroshima, where the atomic bomb was dropped in 1945. Over 200,000 people were killed by the bombs. I want to live in peace and I want my children to live in peace. Please tell us what you think about peace, and please draw an X on the above map to show us where you live."

Unexpectedly, tears came into my eyes, Helene's as well, as we wrote our answers.

I hadn't expected to speak about war among the natural beauties of Kyoto. But here I was forced to think about it again by the daughters of my enemy. On their sheets I wrote about flying a P-51 over Japan many times in World War II, and that I longed for a peaceful world. Helene's message was similar. "I was a young girl when the war started," she wrote, "and about your age when the war ended. I read about Hiroshima in a book by an American author and I remember how sad I felt for anyone who experienced the horrors of war. I, too, want to live in peace and to see my children and their children live in peace as well. We must never allow war to occur again." The mood of our afternoon shifted dramatically as our attention was drawn to the high school students and their project on peace in the world. After we filled in their paper, they handed us a postcard with their names, addresses, and the message of peace written on it.

A few months later, I sent Hisako and Takako an article I had written; the story of my experiences in the war. In time I received the following letter. It came from Tamio Yanagisma, Takako and Hisako's English teacher.

"After we returned from Kyoto last November, I collected fifty-two messages my students had received. I told them that your messages were the most impressive ones we had received. I made a handout of your messages and all 280 students in the class read them. So I was extremely happy when you wrote to my students and enclosed your article. I was not only happy but very moved. Your experience in the war was severe and sad. But now you have discovered that the Japanese are peace-loving people. I was caught by the deep emotions of your story and asked my students to make a booklet, translated by them and me, for the rest of the school. I will send you one when it is completed. A lot of thanks to both of you for giving my students a precious and unforgettable memory on their school trip."

That first week in Japan created confusion and emotions within me that were difficult to deal with. I hadn't expected the welcome by those we encountered or the serenity and beauty we saw. Although I remembered how green the countryside was in the spring and summer of 1945 when I was strafing airfields or trains, I was not prepared for the openness or friendliness of the people we encountered or the stillness I found in the surroundings. Even in Tokyo, with all the noise and bustle, we found small parks and shrines that reverberated in silence.

Back in Tokyo, the concierge in our hotel recommended we see the Festival of the Cranes at a nearby temple. "You are fortunate. The festival is this afternoon. The temple grounds are beautiful this time of year and the Crane Festival is famous all over Japan. Many dancers will imitate the graceful movements of the crane in their mating rites. The crane is a symbolic bird to the Japanese. It is said that the Emperor is the voice of the crane and the dance is a dance of life. We also believe that the crane is the bird that carries our souls to heaven when we die."

"Is the festival far?" Helene asked.

"No, no. Just a few minutes' walk. Come, I will show you the way."

The three of us walked to the street in front of the hotel. The concierge pointed and said, "Two blocks that way, then left three blocks. You will see lots of people there."

The sidewalks were crowded with people, the streets filled with cars and taxicabs. Somehow all seemed orderly. I don't remember hearing any horns blowing. There were no cars in the road on the approach to the temple. The street, instead, was filled with thirty or forty men wearing papier-mâché feathers, weaving, emulating a gyrating bird, as they approached the temple stairs.

As we neared the shrine, I immediately noticed two elderly men in uniform—Japanese soldiers—alongside the steps. One was without arms and had a cup strapped around his neck, for passersby to toss coins into. The other was legless, sitting on his stumps on a blanket.

I was startled for the moment and felt a powerful urge to approach them, an almost overwhelming desire to talk to these soldiers.

It was the strangest feeling, one I had never felt before. I looked at them with pity for their wounds. But there was more. I knew I would feel better if I could talk to them, but I wanted them to talk to me as well. I felt the need to talk about the war with someone who had fought on the other side.

Looking at the crippled veterans, I felt the shame and embarrassment they must have been feeling. Begging is not a dignified pastime for anyone, let alone soldiers, Japanese or American.

Of course, I didn't speak to them. I didn't even go near them. I dropped a few coins into one of the tin boxes and turned aside.

Then, quite suddenly, it struck me. These were the first live Japanese soldiers I had ever seen! Almost instantly I was back on Iwo Jima. The last Japanese soldier I had seen was a dead officer in a cave.

It is common practice to pick up a few souvenirs during wartime: an enemy helmet or bayonet, a flag, part of a uniform. One afternoon on Iwo, a few of us put on our helmets, took a jeep, and drove to an American-held area where I knew a staff sergeant.

"Captain Yellin," he said when we pulled up. "Do you want to see a cave that we've finally captured? We've been trying to take it for days."

"Yes," we all replied eagerly.

We thought we might pick up some souvenirs to take home. And we wanted to see the dead Japs. We wanted to feel that, to know that. Part of being a soldier on Iwo Jima was to go see dead Japs where they were killed. For me, it was a way to at least see the results of somebody else's fighting. As a pilot, I never saw the results of mine.

The sergeant led us past some trees, where we saw the burned, twisted bodies of Japanese soldiers who had been caught by flamethrowers; nothing more was left of them than black shadows in the charred branches.

We had to be careful entering the cave. Because the Japanese knew that Americans would examine the dead bodies for souvenirs, they had a policy of mining their dead. They would attach bombs to the bodies, or bury bombs or mortar shells nearby and stretch thin, almost invisible trip wires between bodies, attached to a belt or belt loop. When the Americans went through the area, they would set off the bombs. The Japanese killed a lot of people this way.

The sergeant led us into a still-smoking entranceway that was partially blocked by a dead soldier, a young officer. The body must have been lying there for some time because the smell in the cave was horrible. The soldier's face was full of maggots. I reached down and pulled the belt on his pants to move the body so that we could pass into the cave. The belt almost went right through the body. I shuddered and let go of it.

Next to the body lay a photograph of a man in full-dress uniform and a little girl—obviously the young officer and his daughter. She was wearing a white dress, her eyes bright under a dark head of hair. Their faces were serious and composed, as the Japanese always prefer to be in pictures.

Despite the almost unbearable stench, we carefully walked deeper inside the cave. I saw a small wooden box and opened it. Among other things it contained a ceremonial knife, wrapped in a piece of cloth.

"That's a *hara-kiri* knife," my Marine friend said. "Do you want to keep it?" I did.

After I got back to my foxhole that night I couldn't sleep. I couldn't even close my eyes. And in later years, when I had recurring dreams of the war, I was always in that cave with the dead Japanese body. Night after night I saw the picture of the man with his daughter—that, and the maggot-filled eyes of the dead soldiers piled up for burial.

I put the *hara-kiri* knife in my footlocker, where it stayed until I took it with me on my return home after the war. That and a blood-stained Japanese flag that I took from a dead soldier's body were the only mementos of the war that I kept.

Of course, the real souvenirs of the war, which I had stored in my mind and carried around with me always, were my memories, those images. Nobody knew about them. I never talked about them to anyone. But I saw these pictures almost every day for years.

CHAPTER 5

Kenrokuen

Hida Takayama is a mountain town famous for its six-hundred-year-old thatched-roof farm village. On our first morning there, we got lost. We were staying at a *ryokan* near the restored village. We walked into the small village and could not remember how to get back to our inn from town.

There were groups of Japanese students everywhere we traveled, sightseeing and having their pictures taken by classmates or by professional photographers. All wore school uniforms, even the youngest ones, those in kindergarten and first grade. They would typically stare at Helene and me, hold up their fingers in a V, and grin as we pointed our camera in their direction.

The older girls sometimes shyly approached us (never singly; always in pairs or more) and asked us to pose with them. They laughed and giggled, holding their hands over their mouths in a delightful gesture of modesty as they thanked us.

We approached a group of five high school students for directions. The students, all boys, huddled together for a moment, then asked us to follow them.

They all started talking at once, in English, and even shouted to their teacher that they were taking the *gai jin* (foreigners) to the village and would meet the class at the bus sometime later.

They were anxious to impress us with their knowledge of America, their language skills, and their pride in the village buildings. When we passed an ice cream stand, we stopped and bought them ice cream, which they pronounced "aisucuremu." They, in turn, bought a small souvenir for Helene—a set of miniature Japanese dolls which she still has, nearly a decade later. The boys even paid for a ticket to an exhibit they wanted us to see.

With all the stops and the animated conversations, the short walk back to our inn took two hours. I couldn't imagine approaching five high school students in America and then following them around for two hours in a strange city! I am not even sure that I would have been so gracious and helpful to foreigners when I was younger, and I'm not proud of that. And these were the children and the grandchildren of the people I had hated.

Our travels also took us to the Kenrokuen, one of Japan's three most famous landscape gardens, situated in Kanazawa, capital of the whole Hokuriku (seacoast) area, seven hours from Tokyo by train.

To the Japanese, a perfect garden consists of six elements: water, size, serenity, space, careful arrangement, and appearance. Kenrokuen has all of these elements, blended in exquisite beauty.

Helene and I spent two days there in the misty rains of late October. We walked on stone pathways through the pine trees, across streams and small lakes with garden islands.

From the front gate, we heard the sound of running water under the small, stone bridge at the entrance and were immediately enchanted. The leaves were changing color, and the gardens were ablaze with red and gold, interspersed with green pine trees. It was early in the morning; rain had fallen the night before and a light fog hung in the air. It seemed as if we were the only people in the entire garden. As we walked across the bridge and entered the garden,

Helene stopped and, overcome with the silence and the exquisite vista, tears forming in her eyes, said, "I have never ever felt or seen such beauty."

Every tree in Kenrokuen is carefully tended and has a life unto itself. It doesn't get lost, as in a forest, but each is cut and pruned to bring out its full beauty and individuality. The park is over one hundred acres in extent, and gravel paths lead in all directions. A beautiful lake spreads out through the park, with many islands in it and huge stepping-stones leading out to them.

The garden had space, and beautiful colors from the changing leaves. It had water, both flowing and still. It had serenity. And best of all, because of the weather, it had solitude and quiet. There was no one there.

While we were walking in the park, Helene told me something that, she said, had been increasingly on her mind during the trip.

"You know, Robert would love this place."

"You mean these gardens?"

"Yes, he would love the gardens. But I'm talking about Japan. He would like the stillness and the beauty that we have felt and seen."

Helene and I met on a blind date on Good Friday, 1949, became engaged on May 30, and were married on October 22. She was only nineteen years old when we were married; I was twenty-five. Our first son, David, was born thirteen months later, followed shortly by Steven, Michael, and Robert, all before we celebrated our tenth anniversary. Helene and I always had a meaningful, close relationship. I can't remember a time in our lives that she wasn't there for me or the children.

She has been my guide to a richer life. When she and Steven began practicing Transcendental Meditation (TM) in August 1975, I resisted her urging to join in meditation until April 1976, when I learned TM. It has been one of the many unifying experiences we have shared in our life together. As we have grown older and our children have moved into their own careers, we have become even closer. I trust her judgment in everything, yet I had never told her about my experiences as a fighter pilot on lwo Jima or over Japan. She never asked and I never offered.

Shortly after we moved to California in 1976, Helene visited Warrens, an oriental antique store in Laguna Beach, with a friend. That night she told me how much she had been affected by what she had seen. "I can't explain the feeling that came over me," she said. "The aesthetics, the lines of the architecture, the shape of the pottery, the screens—everything I saw fascinated me. There seemed to be a connection."

That was the beginning of our small collection of Japanese artifacts and books on gardens. She spent countless hours reading and looking at pictures of Japanese art. Through her influence, we came to own several lovely Japanese antiques, a beautiful screen, some calligraphy, and pottery.

Robert is the youngest of our four sons. David, our oldest son, introduced us to the mood and the sounds of the sixties when he brought Bob Dylan records into our home. In time, we learned to enjoy the music and the poetry, but it wasn't easy. Steven, Michael, and Robert all collected the music of the day as well. From our sons we learned a new language, new philosophies. David began his search for life's meaning at eighteen when he began studying Eastern religions.

As our children were growing, they searched and found a spirituality far beyond what I knew. Helene seemed to sense more of a spiritual feeling in Robert than I did and felt he would resonate with Japan. She often followed her intuition about what she thought her sons would like to read, to see and experience. She was rarely wrong.

"There is a lot here to interest him," she said. "I think we should offer Rob a trip to Japan as a graduation present."

Robert is an unusual young man, someone who has always been very deep and sensitive. I was learning that a spiritual influence permeates the Japanese culture: a love for nature, a sense of oneness, respect, and awe. The thought of my son visiting Japan had never crossed my mind. I didn't respond for a few minutes and finally agreed, "Why not, we can afford it." I had enjoyed my visit so far and was beginning to see Japan in a different light. We decided to suggest it to Robert as soon as we returned to the States.

INDEX